"Can They Do That?"
by
Doug Traubel
CASE LAW & COMMENTARY ON HOW POLICE OFFICERS GET AROUND THE FOURTH AMENDMENT

Amendment IV
"The right of the people to be secure in their persons, houses, papers, and effects, against unreasonable searches and seizures, shall not be violated, and no warrants shall issue, but upon probable cause, supported by oath or affirmation, and particularly describing the place to be searched, and the persons or things to be seized."

When a police officer asks for consent to search your person, house, papers and effects, it is because he has no warrant and no probable cause. An American's default position should be "no." This default position is not because you have anything to hide, but rather as a matter of principle tied to our origins under the abuse of the British Crown.

This publication provides the reader with an understanding of how search and seizure "case law" applies to the streets of America from the peace officer's perspective.

The Orwellian "Patriot Act" and the NDAA (National Defense Authorization Act) have all but destroyed our Fourth Amendment protections from the evolving federal police state.

Under the Patriot Act **without a judge**, the FBI can in essence sign their own search warrants (mostly related to one's activity on the Web) and then leave the recipient with a "national security letter" gag order threatening arrest if the visit/search is revealed.

Under the NDAA you can be detained **indefinitely** without due process and without a trial for committing a "belligerent act." What constitutes a belligerent act is determined unilaterally, without legal representation of the person seized and held.

It is only at the local level between police and the public where the Fourth Amendment has any real relevance, and that relationship is what this admittedly dry read is about.

Some of my brothers and sisters in blue will criticize me for revealing to the public how police operate around the Fourth Amendment. To them I say, "Check your oath."

The majority of case law citied is from the author's home state of Idaho and others are from federal **case** law; most **appear in *italics*.** All states have similar case law, but with their own nuances. **Nothing in this book is intended as legal advice.** Peace officers using the index as a quick (field) reference should always confer with their prosecutor for advice, direction and the most current case law.

In my book, **RED BADGE, *A Veteran Peace Officer's Commentary on the Marxist Subversion of American Law Enforcement and Culture,* I explain why "case law" is a misnomer. Our U.S. Constitution does not give the judicial branch the authority to make law. Nonetheless, it is the accepted and driving force of the unconstitutional Administrative State that lords over us. The more we follow case law, the farther away from the Constitution we drift. **

Excerpts from Red Badge follow this book. One of them touches on the citizens' right as a juror to nullify. Nullification is an effective tool for pushing back government overreach.

DEFINITIONS:
Reasonable Suspicion, (The standard to detain): Is based on the "totality of circumstances." Police may detain based on "...specific and articulable facts that the suspect has been, is, or is about to engage in criminal activity."

Probable Cause (PC) #1, (The standard to arrest): "...information that would lead a person of ordinary care and prudence (good judgment) to entertain an honest and strong suspicion that the person arrested has committed a crime."

Probable Cause (PC) #2, (The standard for a search warrant): PC to issue a search warrant is determined by evaluating the totality of circumstances and making a "Practical, common-sense decision whether, given all the circumstances set forth in the affidavit before {the magistrate}, including the *veracity* (reliability/credibility) and 'basis of knowledge' of persons supplying hearsay information, contraband or evidence of a crime will be found in a particular place."

Investigative detentions are an essential part of effective, proactive police work.

Being a professional requires that police officers know and follow the rules for detaining subjects and searching them for weapons. These rules come from federal case law in Terry v. Ohio.

TERRY V. OHIO
An investigative detention requires reasonable suspicion defined above. Although reasonable suspicion is enough to stop and investigate, it is *not* enough to search for weapons.

A Terry pat down (also called "stop and frisk") requires three things:
1) Reasonable Suspicion (grounds for the investigative stop)
2) Officer reasonably believes the subject is armed
3) Officer has an immediate concern for his safety

Idaho law (State v. Wright, A., 134 Idaho 73,996 P.2d 292 (2000): and Fleenor) does not require police be absolutely certain the subject is armed and dangerous. The standard is the totality of circumstances from which the officer infers the subject was armed AND dangerous. Idaho law (State v. Muir, 116 Idaho 565,777 P.2d 1238 (Ct. App. 1989) holds police to an objective and subjective standard.

Objectively, would a reasonable person in the officer's situation believe the subject was armed <u>and</u> dangerous? Remember, believing the subject is armed is not enough: Armed and dangerous is the standard. Someone police contact that is merely open carrying a gun or knife is not justification to search or disarm.

Subjectively, at the time of the frisk, did the officer actually have an immediate concern for his safety or the safety of others?

<u>**Note**</u>: During a Terry pat down the ***Plain Feel Doctrine*** allows police to seize non-threatening items if its incriminating character is "...immediately apparent to touch." An officer cannot use continued manipulation of the item if he has ruled out a weapon.

Search of a container on suspect's person during a Terry pat down was lawful when suspect admitted it contained drugs. This admission switched the search authority from Terry to a broader scope based on Probable Cause – to search for contraband.

TERRY SEARCH ON A CONSENSUAL CONTACT

Can an officer do a Terry pat down for weapons on a consensual contact? Yes, provided two of the three requirements for stop and frisk are present:
- Officer believes the subject is armed
- Officer has an immediate concern for his safety

During a consensual encounter the subject answers in the affirmative to the officer's question about having any weapons on him. This alone is not enough to frisk. (State v. Henage, 143 Idaho 655, 152 p.3d (2007). Police must articulate an immediate concern for their safety.

A citizen lawfully exercising his Second Amendment Right to open carry sometimes results in officers overreacting.

Scenario:
> Police enter a house with the subject's consent and then develop grounds for a Terry pat down.

A pat down in this situation is lawful. Too often officers are afraid of generating a complaint. This causes them to under react and get hurt. Knowing the guardrails of case law is liberating because officers can act with greater confidence.

FLIGHT

Mere flight is enough to detain, but it is not enough to arrest for *R&O* (resisting and obstructing an officer in the performance of his duties). Illinois v. Wardlow, 5428 U.S. 119,120 S. Ct. 673 (2000).

If an officer gives chase and the subject stops and lets him conduct business there is no crime. The officer being out of breath and mad does not change this fact. On the other hand, if the subject stops and squares off with the officer to fight or resists a *police lead* (a two-handed escort hold), or lies about his identity, it turns to a crime. The subject has a duty to submit to police authority when there is a *legitimate* investigative stop.

Police can make a warrantless entry into a residence to complete a Terry Stop (State v. Manthei, 130 Idaho 237, 939 P.2d 556 (1997). Obviously, this could be quite dangerous for many reasons including the likely animated objection by the subject who may be operating under a King's X mentality.

Similarly, an officer with probable cause to arrest for a misdemeanor or felony in a public place can make warrantless entry into a residence if the suspect flees inside.

TERRY SEARCHES OF VEHICLES

A Terry pat down of a subject outside of a vehicle may extend to the passenger compartment when the subject has access to weapons inside the automobile (i.e. a rifle in a rack, or saddle bags on a motorcycle). *However, the vehicle must be located within the subject's lunge area. Michigan V. Long, 463 U.S. 1032, 103 S. Ct. 3469 (1983).

Scenario:
> Driver is evasive and fidgety. He continues to move his hands to his waist when told not to. Police believe he could be trying to access a weapon. Police order him out of the car.

Police may frisk him and then search the lunge area under a limited scope for weapons.

Note: A weapon "concealed" means, "...not enough to be discernible by ordinary observer." For example, this includes between the seats, i.e., the butt of a gun sticking out.

Suspect arrested 15 feet from his backpack. Search of the backpack was unlawful. There was no PC to search it and no reasonable suspicion to search it under Terry given it was outside the lunge area (too far away to pose a possible threat). If he denies ownership police may search it as abandoned property.

Officer saw a syringe protruding from driver's pocket. Driver and passenger were removed from the car. Passenger compartment was searched, including passenger's purse where drugs were found: Good search based on PC.

Scenario:
> Officer has reasonable suspicion to detain gang members for fighting in a park. It appears as though he arrived at the close of a jumping-in initiation for a new member. The detained

subjects are within lunge distance of a car that is associated with and/or frequently driven by members of the gang.

In addition to doing a frisk for weapons of all of the subjects there police can do a search of the car limited to weapons.

Problem:
With the exception of scenarios like the one above, procedurally, on a traffic stop, once an officer removes someone from a car and sits him on the curb he has placed the subject physically at a disadvantage from lunging and perhaps even outside of the lunge area. This may make it more difficult for the officer to articulate meeting the requirements of a Terry search on the car. However, if the subject continues to move closer to the car disobeying reasonable and necessary commands to not move, the officer may have stronger grounds to act accordingly within the three requirements for a Terry search of the car.

On a traffic stop an officer can only search the car for weapons if he sincerely has a concern that it contains a weapon and has immediate concern for his safety.

Officers should always be checking their motive. Honoring one's oath is what separates police from the criminal. "Mr. Big" might drive off with the dope under his seat, but it is better that he get away today than police break the rules to search his car. Police need to be digging for crime by making lots of good contacts, not by stretching the rules of search and seizure and compromising their oath.

Every contact police make either builds or erodes trust and confidence in the eyes of the law-abiding population and the criminal. The reality is that police need credibility with both camps. I know that it is difficult to let someone go when an officer's gut tells him there is contraband in the car, but police must follow the rules because they are bound by their oath.

An internal monologue is helpful for an officer to regulate his conduct within the guardrails of the case law governing each of these three kinds of contacts:

- **Consensual**: requires the consent of the party contacted

- **Detention**: requires Reasonable Suspicion

- **Arrest**: requires Probable Cause (PC)

Furthermore, it is a good practice for an officer to tell the citizen his status. For example, "You are not under arrest. I am detaining you while I sort out what is going on here. Have a seat." If the subject runs after being told this, then probable cause to arrest for *resisting and obstructing an officer in the performance of his duties* is stronger in light of the clear communication with him at the onset over his detention status.

1. CONSENT CONTACTS

During a Consent Contact an officer may ask for identification and may ask to search. The citizen can refuse. An officer should not take offense when a citizen asserts his right. While this may frustrate an officer — contempt of cop is not a crime. Remember, the right of The People to be *free from* government intrusion.

Motorist assists should be treated as consent contacts unless the officer develops reasonable suspicion or PC to do otherwise.

A vehicle legally parked on the side of the road with a subject inside need NOT give police his driver license although they may ask for it. This is a consent contact. If police stop behind it with only their rear amber lights on, it is still a consent contact, but if the blue forward-facing light is on case law tells us this is an unlawful detention.

2. DETENTIONS
Detentions require responsible suspicion to make. **Mere flight IS grounds for an investigative detention.** The cause and effect relationship of a person seeing a uniformed police officer and instantly fleeing does support reasonable suspicion. Illinois v. Wardlow, 528 U.S. 119,120 S. Ct. 673 (2000) and In re Deen, 131 Idaho 435, 958 P.2d 592 (1998). This can turn into an arrest depending whether or not the person ultimately detained physically resists police in the process or obstructs his investigation with lies.

"Excessively cautious driving" can be among reasons for investigative detention i.e. the car and occupant(s) generally match the description of suspect(s) & vehicle of a fresh crime nearby and follow every traffic law perfectly when police are following them. Police rely here on the *totality of circumstances* to articulate reasonable suspicion.

Officers cannot make an investigative stop for *DWP* (driving without privilege /suspended license) **unless** the physical description of the driver matches more specifically than gender alone.

Scenario:
> An officer runs a vehicle registration check on a license plate and then runs a driver license check on the registered owner of the vehicle. The officer learns the registered owner of the vehicle has a suspended driving privilege.

Police cannot stop the car unless the person driving the car matches the description of the person with the suspended privilege. For example, if the owner of the car has a suspended license and is white, but the driver of the car is a black, police have no reason to believe that the driver of the car is the actual owner with the suspended driving privilege. The owner might have let someone drive his car.

Reasonable Suspicion can be formed by *collective knowledge* of all officers involved in an investigation to support an investigative stop i.e. a recent police bulletin, or radio traffic among multiple officers updating information about a crime they are working. (See Page and 24 for transferring PC to another officer. Do not confuse the two.)

Anonymous tips alone are not enough to support reasonable suspicion. The officer needs to add his own observations to what an anonymous tipster or reliable tipster provides for there to be a foundation of reasonable suspicion.

Police should consider the possibility of a hidden agenda of an anonymous reporting party. In the course of my career citizens have tried to use me as a pawn to harass a neighbor or former spouse by reporting bogus information.

In contrast, the following case law does give weight to a reporting party that identifies himself to dispatch.

STATE v. VAN DORNE
STATE of Idaho, Plaintiff-Respondent, v. Dawn Jeanine VAN DORNE, Defendant-Appellant.
No. 29379.
March 16, 2004

This Court has stated that where the information comes from a known citizen informant rather than an anonymous tipster, the citizen's disclosure of her identity, which carries the risk of accountability if the allegations turn out to be fabricated, is generally deemed adequate to show veracity and reliability.

See State v. Alexander, 138 Idaho 18, 24, 56 P.3d 780, 786 (Ct.App.2002); Larson, 135 Idaho at 101, 15 P.3d at 336. A known citizen is one who provides facts from which his or her identity can be readily ascertained. Larson, 135 Idaho at 102, 15 P.3d at 337.

Even with the above case law, we need to measure the circumstances described by the known citizen (Reporting Party) against the definition of reasonable suspicion.

Scenario:

> Police are dispatched to a known citizen's report of an "armed subject." The reporting party is Professor Sanchez who reported a white male wearing a t-shirt that says, "Stop the Invasion" on the front and "Minute Man" on the back. The subject is said to be wearing a sidearm in plain view walking down a public sidewalk by the university.

Based on this information alone there are no grounds to detain. The professor's hope or expectation is that police detain the subject and prone him out. But all we have here is one citizen reporting another citizen for exercising his First and Second Amendment rights simultaneously (a T-shirt with a political statement and a gun). Police cannot allow the perception, hidden agenda or intolerance of the professor to fuel a politically correct, illegal detention. In this case there are three options for the officer: (1) Advise the professor of the facts of life in a free society and go "*10-8*" (back in service), (2) Observe the armed subject at a distance or perhaps by using an available plain-clothes unit in order to assess his candid behavior, or (3) attempt a consent contact. Had the call been properly screened it should NOT have been dispatched, but rather only broadcasted as "area information" to officers.

TRAFFIC STOPS
Driving through 3 intersections with a turn signal on is sufficient for a traffic stop to investigate inattentive driving.

*An investigative stop of a car with out-of-state plates can be made (for failure to register within 90 days) **if** an officer is familiar with the driver and car enough to know sufficient time has passed.*

*Only a **severely** cracked windshield is a vehicle equipment violation in Idaho (IC 49-902 (1)), not small cracks and chips. Remember the **spirit of the law** and use good judgment.*

Police cannot make a stop for a vehicle code violation and then – without reasonable suspicion – question occupants about drug possession. (State vs. Myers 118 Idaho 608,798 p.2d 453 (ct.app.1990).

How offended would an off-duty officer be if he/she was questioned about drug use or possession without reasonable cause? Sometimes when off duty I know that I look a little rough unshaven in my "Mr. Fix It" clothes and driving my old pickup. That doesn't make me a doper.

PC existed when a credible CI (confidential informant) said suspect would be driving from point A to point B in a yellow car with a gun and drugs. The vehicle registration showed that the suspect owned a yellow car. CI picked suspect out of a photo lineup. On the

date the CI said, the suspect was driving the expected route. **Good stop and search.**
A traffic stop on a subject leaving a house where a controlled drug buy just took place is a good investigative traffic stop.

Officers can order passengers out of a car even if they are not involved in criminal activity and the situation appears normal and benign, Maryland v. Wilson, 519 U.S. 408, 117 S. Ct. 882 (1997). Police should not abuse this. Police should check their motive when they order an occupant out of the car. "**Are my actions ethical, necessary and reasonable?**"

Handcuffing the driver and/or passenger does not convert the contact into an arrest State v. Wright, E., 134 Idaho 79, 996 P.2d 298 (2000). This action can be based on the totality of circumstances i.e. the person's intimidating, uncooperative behavior, furtive movement, and hyper-nervousness can all be used to articulate the well-founded reasons for cuffing to control the contact for officer safety. Frisking the subject for weapons first and then doing a search of the car limited to weapons is reasonable because presumably he will be released from handcuffs and free to return to the car (at the conclusion of the contact) where a weapon could be waiting.

Officers should make it a practice to tell the citizen his status when cuffing. Tell him he is being detained and is not under arrest and why he is being cuffed: "Your behavior is causing me concern for my safety. You are not under arrest, but I am detaining you. Turn around...." Granted, there may not be time for conversation until after the officer restores order in a chaotic scene by cuffing the apparent threat first. In either case, everyone deserves an explanation.

There are times when police have good reason to do a Terry pat down, but fail to articulate it to the person searched or in the police report resulting in a suppression hearing and/or an internal affairs complaint. This makes an officer's intentions look less than honorable to the courts and public we serve.

Even after the original grounds for an investigative traffic stop have dissipated the officer may continue to detain the driver to get Driver License, Insurance and Registration.

Scenario:
> Police pull a car over for no plates and then determine there is a valid temporary registration on the rear window. Police can still run a registration check, driver license check and warrants check, and demand driver's license and proof of insurance.

2(B) PRETEXT STOPS

*If police have reasonable, objective grounds for the traffic stop any underlying motive to stop the subject, as pretext to search for drugs is irrelevant. (Pg. I-26 State vs. Law, 115 Idaho 769,769 9.2d1141 (ct. app 1989). In other words, if police are doing surveillance on a subject's house for suspicion of drug sales or gang related crime and he drives off and know his driving privilege is suspended, they can stop him. Even though their primary interest is another kind of crime, the charge of DWP (driving without privileges) would stand on its own; therefore the pretext is not a problem. The same goes for bald tires or any other valid violation for a stop. The general public confuses this with what the media spin as "profiling."

Pretext stops are lawful so long as there is an objectively reasonable ground to make the traffic stop. Ulterior motives are irrelevant.

DISTINGUISHING THE CHIMEL RULE FROM TERRY
Do not blur the line of case law between Chimel and Terry. A Terry search is limited to weapons only. **Chimel is case law tied to probable cause** (arrest). Chimel allows police to search for weapons **and** evidence within the lunge area, i.e. beer cans in a car related to a DUI arrest (Idaho v. Cantrell). ***The search can be made before or after the physical arrest.***

Terry is tied to reasonable suspicion. It relates *only* to officer safety and allows police to look exclusively for weapons only in places where they could reasonably be found and accessible. Chimel is tied to probable cause and gives broader search authority.

2(C) PROTECTIVE SEARCHES OF VEHICLES
Police may search the passenger compartment limited to places a weapon may be hidden if:
- Police have made a lawful stop
- Police reasonably believe the subject is armed and poses danger to the officer and/or

- Police reasonably believe the subject may gain immediate control of weapon in car

Police can search a car for weapons if the subject is outside of it. The court recognizes that the subject could run to the car and arm himself and/or go to it after he is released and harm officers. Contraband found in plain view during a weapons search is lawful to seize and charge.

Scenario:
Police respond to a property damage collision. One of the parties is belligerent toward the officer(s) and has prison tattoos, suggesting a criminal past. In the car on the floorboard the officer sees a roofing hammer. The subject hears the officer running a warrant check and driver license check on him. He fails to stay where the officer told him to stand and moves toward the car.

If based on behavioral cues and/or failure to obey reasonable and necessary orders to stay put, police believe he may be moving to a position of advantage to arm himself police may pat him down and search the car for weapons.

If under this scenario police search the car first for weapons and find contraband anywhere a weapon might have been, the officer will likely lose it in a suppression hearing. Why? Answer: If the officer truly felt concerned for his safety he would have begun with a frisk of the subject and then the car — in that order.

2 (D) PROTECTIVE SWEEPS

Police may search areas immediately adjoining the area of arrest — where an attack could be launched Buie, 494 U.S. at 334.

Police can search closets and other spaces immediately adjoining the place of arrest provided, *"...that the search must be narrowly confined to a "cursory inspection of those spaces where a person may be found." Id. at 335. Further, the sweep may last "no longer than is necessary to dispel the reasonable suspicion of danger and in any event no longer than it takes to complete the arrest and depart the premises."* Id. at 335–36.

Usually these sweeps are done when executing a search warrant or arrest warrant, but if an officer responds to a crime of violence like domestic battery, murder, robbery or kidnap he may be able to articulate a sweep for additional victims/suspects.

During a protective sweep police may seize evidence seen in **plain view**. Police will need a search warrant to search for additional evidence not in plain view.

Although Buie involved an in-home arrest, courts have applied the doctrine when police are executing a search warrant so as to allow a protective sweep of areas beyond the boundaries allowed by the warrant. State v. Schaffer, 133 Idaho 126, 982 P.2d 961.
Further clarification on the expansion of protective sweeps is found in: State of Idaho, Plaintiff–Respondent, v. Arnoldo ROJAS–TAPIA, Defendant–Appellant.No. 37582. August 10, 2011

FACTS AND PROCEDURE
In September 2009, Officer Scott Ward was executing a search warrant on premises in Gooding County, where it was believed a small marijuana grow was being conducted. Specifically, the search warrant was for a trailer on the premises identified as "Trailer B" and the property around that trailer. Officer Ward later testified that prior to execution of the warrant, officers did not know who lived at the residence or if the occupants had any weapons or dogs, but believed there to be at least two to three people living in the trailer.

When Officer Ward and others arrived to execute the warrant they saw a Hispanic male, later identified as Arnoldo Rojas–Tapia, outside Trailer B in a "garden area." While Officer Ward and another officer were "securing" Rojas–Tapia, they observed two other Hispanic males exiting what was described as a "rock building" on the premises, approximately ten yards from Trailer B. The two men were handcuffed, searched, and removed to the front of the house. According to Officer Ward's testimony, in order to "secure the scene" and ensure officer safety, several officers entered the rock building to "make sure there was nobody in it" and that no one would come out of the building brandishing a gun. Inside the rock building, officers noticed multiple drying marijuana plants. Officer Ward then obtained a search warrant for the rock building and the subsequent search uncovered approximately forty hanging marijuana plants...

... Turning to the facts of the case, the court noted several factors: The distance between Trailer B (described in the warrant) and the rock building was approximately 10 yards; Detective Ward had over

twenty years' experience in narcotics investigations and testified that, based on this experience, those involved in narcotics often carry guns;

Given the fact that officers had observed two males exit the Rock Building at the time of execution of the search warrant, and given [the] location and proximity of the Rock House to the area where the defendant and others were being detained, a reasonable and prudent law enforcement officer would take precautions to make sure that no other individuals were located within the Rock Building.

Accordingly, we conclude that the officers possessed the requisite articulable facts which, taken together with the rational inferences from those facts, would warrant a reasonably prudent officer in believing that the area to be swept harbors an individual posing a danger to those on the premises—namely that the persons present on the premises were suspected of drug activity, persons involved in drug activity often carried guns...

2(D) 1. PROTECTIVE FRISK

When executing a search warrant police may detain and handcuff anyone there in order to control the scene. However, police may search them for weapons **_only_** if they have reasonable suspicion that they are armed. An officer's training and experience play a big part in articulating reasonable suspicion to search for weapons. For instance, while serving a search warrant on a SUREÑO XIII gang house it is reasonable that anyone present wearing gang attire could be armed. Police know this based on their training and experience.

It is important that the officer elaborate on this in his report.

On the other hand, arresting Dan the Doper in his Aunt Mabel's house does not allow police to search her for weapons "just because."
Safety Tip: When rounding up the occupants police should search the sofa and chairs for weapons *before* sitting the detained subject(s) down on it.

3. ARRESTS
An arrest is a seizure of a person. It is defined by **detention + significant movement**. This is why police bring the witness to the suspect where he is being detained for a *field show-up* (identification) and not the other way around *(unless the witness is badly injured and cannot be transported). A field-show-up is also known as a curbside lineup. It is when a witness is brought to a detained person an asked to make or exclude identification.

Warrantless arrests are presumptively illegal. The exceptions to the arrest warrant requirement are statutory, unlike the exceptions to warrantless searches that are based upon case law.

Evidence or contraband discovered after a warrantless arrest cannot be used retroactively to strengthen the grounds for the arrest. If the officer did not have PC before the arrest, then anything found or learned thereafter cannot be retroactively applied to strengthen his foundation (fruit of the poisonous tree).

One officer may transfer PC to another officer so long as the crime is a felony. State v. Oakley, 119 Idaho 1006, 812 P.2d 313 (Ct. App. 1991) and Idaho Code 19-603 (3).

If radio communication between officers is the only grounds for the arrest, then the communication itself must be based upon reliable information strong enough to establish PC.

3(A). MISDEMEANORS NOW REQUIRING A CITIZEN'S ARREST IF NOT COMMITTED IN OFFICER'S PRESENCE:

- Assault and battery when police response is immediately following the event (IC 19-603)

- Domestic Battery

- Violation of Protection Orders, NCOs and second degree stalking

- Helping with a citizen's arrest (for example, but not limited to a store loss prevention agent wrestling with a shoplifter)

- Drug Offenses IC 37-2740 (3)

- Fish and Game Violations

- Status Offenses i.e. tobacco, curfew, juvenile beyond control

- Misdemeanors committed by juveniles

- Any crime aboard an aircraft

- Motor vehicle offenses listed under IC 49-1405

IDAHO CODE 49-1405: ARRESTS FOR SERIOUS OFFENSES. (1) The authority to make an arrest is the same as it would be for a felony when any person is charged with any of the following offenses:

A.   Negligent homicide.
B.   Driving, or being in actual physical control, of a vehicle or operating a vessel while under the influence of alcohol or other intoxicating beverage.
C.   Driving a vehicle or operating a vessel while under the influence of any narcotic drug, or driving a vehicle or operating a vessel while under the influence of any other drug to a degree which renders the person incapable of safely driving a vehicle.
D.   Failure to stop, or failure to give information, or failure to render reasonable assistance, in the event of an accident resulting in death or personal injuries.
E.   Failure to stop, or failure to give information, in the event of an accident resulting in damage to a vehicle or vessel or to fixtures or other property legally upon or adjacent to a highway or waterway.
F.   Reckless driving.
G.   Fleeing or attempting to elude a peace officer.

Misdemeanor DUI is treated like a felony for purpose of investigation and arrest (State v. Ruhter, 107 Idaho 282, 688 p.2d 1187 (1984)

An officer can arrest for a misdemeanor attempted or continued in his presence. For example, an officer can arrest for driving without privileges (DWP) when it is attempted in his presence.

Scenario:
An officer cited a driver last week for DWP. This week falls within the effective dates of the suspension and the officer sees him walking toward a car. The officer observes the suspect open the driver door, sit in the driver seat, close the door and put on his seat belt.

Without letting him drive the officer could cite him for attempting to drive while DWP. The standard is, would a reasonable person believe he was about to drive?

Scenario:
The manager at a movie theater told the suspect to leave, but he refused. On the manager's behalf the officer tells suspect to leave and he refuses.

Although the original crime was not committed in the officer's presence, the continuation of the crime was. The officer may arrest for trespass committed in his presence.

3(B) WARRANTLESS ENTRY
Police may enter residence to affect arrest (including motel room) when:
- PC is established in a public place for a felony or misdemeanor and suspect flees inside
- Hot pursuit
- Exigency i.e. police hear screaming, or see smoke
- Consent i.e. any person with "*apparent authority*" (See Page 36). For example, the live-

in girlfriend of a Domestic Violence suspect gives police consent to enter.

Police can only make warrantless entry if the contact began outside the residence.

Example: Police knock on door of apartment "A." The tenant of apartment "B" opens the door and the officer smells the odor of marijuana and/or sees paraphernalia in plain view inside. Police cannot make a warrantless entry of apartment "B" **because the contact did not begin outside**. Furthermore, the evidence is of non-violent crime. State v. Curl, 125 Idaho 224, 869 P.2d 224 (1993).

Police cannot force entry to suspect's home to arrest for DUI where a citizen reports it and there was no fresh pursuit.

*Police can do so if on his own investigative traffic stop the defendant goes inside the residence.

On a misdemeanor arrest warrant police can trick defendant outside and arrest him in a public place. ***Normally misdemeanor arrest warrants cannot be served in the home between the hours of *8:00 PM and 08:00 AM.**

NOTE: On a warrantless misdemeanor arrest, if defendant opens his door and is standing in the threshold police CAN arrest him. If he flees inside police can chase him and arrest him inside.

4. PLAIN VIEW DOCTRINE & OPEN VIEW DOCTRINE

Plain View applies to **warrantless <u>seizures</u>** of items in a constitutionally protected area. Police may seize contraband if it is in plain view inside your home. For example, officers are in your home investigating a domestic battery and see child pornography. They may seize it. They would need to get a search warrant to search for more contraband of that nature.

Open View applies to **warrantless <u>searches</u>** from a location open to the public. If an officer is on the 3rd floor of a hotel building and looks out the window below into the backyard of a house where there are marijuana plants, the search is legal.

*Sense-enhancing technology may constitute a search (expect a suppression hearing). Using thermal imaging from inside *curtilage* is unlawful.

Curtilage: "Area immediately surrounding and associated with a residence in which a person has a reasonable expectation of privacy."

Custom and terrain is a variable in defining curtilage. A rancher's broken fence and one no trespassing sign is not curtilage. The officer could go on the property.

Open Fields doctrine encompasses the unoccupied areas outside the curtilage. Fences and signs do not — per se —create a reasonable expectation of privacy. The absence of gates and no trespassing signs give implied invitation to enter through the normal path to the door. An officer looking in cars through the windows on the way to the house is lawful under the open view doctrine.

Because the car is not on a public road officers would need a search warrant to seize contraband discovered in open view. Under federal law officers could seize it without a warrant, but Idaho Courts have not ruled on this. *(A state can always give more protection to its citizens than the fed. It would be wise to get a search warrant in this circumstance).

5. WARRANTLESS SEARCHES

It is difficult to form a coherent policy on searching because the road map of exceptions to a search warrant is found in a labyrinth of case law.

Like warrantless arrests, warrantless searches violate the 4th Amendment. **As a general rule all warrantless searches and arrests are presumed illegal** UNLESS the state can prove the warrantless action clearly fell within the established exceptions and that it was impractical to obtain a warrant. The measuring stick to search based on PC without a warrant is the *Magistrate Standard*: *An officer's assessment of probable cause must be based on objective facts which would be sufficient to persuade a magistrate to issue a warrant under similar circumstances.*

The following are the exceptions where police may make a warrantless search:

5 (A) AUTOMOBILE EXCEPTION

Passenger(s) and driver have a reduced expectation of privacy with property transported in vehicles. There is an inherent exigency in the potential destruction of evidence due to the mobility of a vehicle.

Police may search any containers; packages or compartments in a vehicle capable of concealing the object of the search provided:
- There is PC to believe the vehicle contains evidence of a crime and
- The vehicle is "readily mobile" (think of an obviously broken down car on private property as a storage shed shaped like a car).

A motor home connected to power is a gray area, depending how long it has been there (police should consult their on-call prosecutor).

IMPORTANT: Officers must not confuse PC to search for a specific item with PC to search the entire car, trunk and all.

The object of the search defines the scope of the search. If police are looking for a stolen bicycle they cannot open the glove box.

If an officer has PC to search a suitcase in the trunk for marijuana this does not give him the broader scope to search the passenger compartment. Police can call for a drug dog. If the dog alerts, a broader search can be made.

Note: There is no expectation of privacy to open a vehicle door and inspect the VIN # or to look on the dashboard for the same.

An officer's authority to search a container is not affected by apparent or expressed belonging to a passenger or third party. But the officer's authority to search does not extend to the body of a third party or passenger.

To be clear, police can order passengers out of the car, but they may not search them for contraband. Merely being there when the driver is arrested is not PC to search the passenger(s). Police can search **anything left** in the car i.e. purses provided the item(s) being searched for could be contained within the area or container searched.

IMPORTANT: Officers cannot order a passenger to leave a purse, backpack or the like in the car, but once they have stepped out and ask to retrieve it officers can deny them and it is included in the search.

*Odor of alcoholic beverage gives police PC to search for open containers.

Officer seized a t-shirt in **plain view** *from inside a vehicle that was stopped during a burglary investigation. This is a lawful seizure. Officer had reasonable suspicion for the investigative stop.*

Scenario:
> Reporting party called dispatch that a car just left a house where a burglary appears to have happened and police make an investigative stop. The behavior of the occupant(s) on the stop support a Terry pat down while detaining them.

Officers should make the stop safe and then slow down. Wait for other officers to verify PC for the burglary at the scene **before** broadening the search for burglary tools, and stolen property. Officers should not jump the gun. They should make the contact safe first and then wait for an update from the officer who is on-scene. *If police do not have PC *before* the search, then what they find — no matter how damning — will not be admissible.

TRUNKS
A minimal amount of contraband i.e. drugs in the passenger compartment does not get police in the trunk.

On the other hand, if police have PC to search the trunk and find something there it may not broaden their search to include the passenger compartment. Call for a drug dog.

When police make a search incident to arrest out of a car remember that the Chimel rule does not get them into the trunk. The scope of their search is limited to where evidence of the crime *could be* found and where weapons could be found in the passenger compartment. Chimel keeps police out of the trunk. That said, some cars (a particular BMW comes to mind) have a rear seat armrest that pulls down and gives a tunnel-like access to the trunk. In this case police can extend their search to the trunk. If they develop PC that evidence is in the trunk they can use the automobile exception to search without a warrant.

More on trunks:
See vehicle inventory searches (Pages 39).

TEMPORAL ISSUE
The search of the car does not have to occur at the same time as the seizure. The same applies to containers within. Police can search it at the scene or later at the station once the car is legally seized.

A suspect is arrested for passing fraudulent checks. His car can be searched at the station.

Arresting a suspect from his car and taking his briefcase at the same time— to be searched later— is fine.

5 (B) SEARCHES INCIDENT TO ARREST
With the important exception of case law in Arizona V. Gant (below), police may search the area around the arrestee's immediate control *including open or closed containers for weapons, contraband and evidence of the crime. The area of search is limited, but the scope is not (Chimel).

CITIZEN'S ARREST
(IC 19-614 Duty of private person making arrest). Police may search an arrestee delivered to him by a citizen. The initial burden of proof for PC is on the citizen. In this case police can search for weapons and contraband without ascertaining if actual PC exists i.e. shoplifters.

Note: After the search, but before taking custody the officer does have the responsibility to assure the citizen had PC for the arrest.

A search can precede the arrest so long as the reason for the search is not based on what was found. Example: Police stop a burglary suspect. The car he is driving matches the description. The witness positively identifies him. Police have PC for the arrest, but have not told the suspect he is under arrest, nor have police cuffed him. Police search the suspect and find evidence of the crime and then arrest him: lawful search, but awful officer safety! (Why didn't the officer(s) tell the suspect his status and handcuff him *before* the search?)

Police should have an internal monologue when searching. Ask, "Under what authority am I acting? What is the scope of my search?" Contacts are fluid and police need to be thinking and searching within the constitutional guardrails and case law.

Defendant cannot defeat officer's authority to search car by hastily separating himself from the car after the officer initiates contact.

Scenario:
>Suspect hurries into a convenience store upon police contacting him and then returns standing near the car.
>Police can still search the car incident to the arrest (unless Gant applies).

ARIZONA V. GANT
This case deals with search incident to arrest from a vehicle for a crime for which there is no physical evidence. It prevents what is commonly referred to by defense attorneys, a "fishing expedition." There is no physical evidence in a charge for driving without privileges. Likewise, there is no physical evidence for an arrest warrant, so there can be no search of the car incident to arrest in such circumstances. However, if police develop PC for a search *unrelated* to the arrest i.e. they smell marijuana then they can press on and search.

5 (C) CONSENT SEARCHES
"Consent may be manifested by words, gesture or conduct."
Consent must be given freely and the person giving it must have the "apparent authority" to give it.

Consent maybe revoked. If the subject is screaming, "stop" from the back seat of the patrol car, officers should do not pretend they can't hear him. Police would be no better than the Crown's soldiers who abused the colonialists if they do not respect the rights our Founding Fathers gave "The People" to be free from unlawful search.

Co-owners and co-tenants can give consent **but** only to the common areas; not areas under the consenter's exclusive control.

Police have no duty to take steps to find a potentially objecting co-tenant.

Unless the tenant *abandons* the premises the landlord has no authority to permit a search. "Abandon" does not mean owing rent. If the tenant moved things out, made statements about being out of there and/or terminated the utilities...Totality of circumstances can support what constitutes "abandoned."

APPARENT AUTHORITY
So long as the officer believed the person giving consent had authority he is on solid ground, even if later it turns out that the person giving consent did not have the authority. For example, a girlfriend with a key to the apartment lets police in. Police then arrest the male half for domestic battery. If it turns out she is not on the lease, no problem.

An employer can give third-party consent to search employee's hard drive, <u>Quom v. Arch</u> *wireless operating Co. INC 529 F.3d 892 (9th cirt-2008)*, but government employees have an expectation of privacy on employer's computer.

<u>Scenario</u>:
> Roommate invites police in. Police smell marijuana coming from the other roommate's room. This is not a common area. Furthermore, this is a non-violent misdemeanor.

The roommate has an expectation of privacy in his room. Police cannot force entry to recover evidence of a non-violent misdemeanor in Idaho.

<u>BAC</u> (Blood, Alcohol Content): Drivers give their implied consent to submit to a BAC test when they get behind the wheel. Until December of 2014 "Forced blood draws" were lawful in Idaho (Idaho Supreme Court. State v. Diaz, 144 Idaho 300, 160 P.3d 739 (Idaho 2007)), without a search warrant, but gratefully the policy of most law enforcement agencies tempered this with restraint – only allowing it when part of an Aggravated DUI or vehicular manslaughter case. Don't get me wrong, a DUI arrest is one of the best arrests police can make; it saves lives. This 2014 ruling was refreshing to see. Police can make a strong enough case on a standard misdemeanor DUI without subjecting citizens to this level of force routinely.

Note: A probationer on unsupervised probation is still subject to warrantless search by a parole officer based on RS, (State v. Klinger, 143 Idaho 494,148 P.3d 1240 (2006) their consent is a condition of probation.

5 (D) EXIGENT CIRCUMSTANCES EXCEPTION
Exigent: "A compelling need for immediate official action and no time to secure a warrant" (Michigan v. Tyler).

However, police may enter without a warrant provided they can articulate the ***immediate need*** for a protective sweep to preserve life or prevent destruction of evidence (of a violent crime). Examples: Murder, domestic violence in progress, fire, and fleeing violent felon. Once the scene is secure and there is a need to look for and collect evidence not in plain view, police should secure the scene and consider a search warrant.

The scope of search cannot exceed the need created by the exigent circumstance.

Example: Police may follow EMS into a place and seize items in plain view so long as EMS are still tending to the exigent circumstance i.e. EMS in a motel room on an overdose and police seize a *hype kit* (intravenous drug paraphernalia).

5 (E) OTHER CIRCUMSTANCES WHEN POLICE CAN ENTER RESIDENCE WITHOUT A SEARCH WARRANT:

- Hot pursuit of fleeing felon OR misdemeanor suspect
- Arrest is initiated outside and defendant retreats inside
- On a valid Terry stop initiated in a public place and suspect retreats into residence to avoid detention
- Consent

Officer may make warrantless entry to prevent the destruction of evidence provided the underlying crime is of a violent nature. i.e. murder, rape, robbery... See section 5 (I) under Fresh Pursuit.

Scenario:

It is a blistering hot summer day. The defendant is under surveillance for murder and just arrived at his mother's home with a gym bag. Police notice smoke coming from the chimney. He could be destroying evidence.

Is there time for a warrant? No.

Absent the exceptions above officers need to hold a perimeter and get a search warrant.
*Police cannot create the exigency by knocking on the door or other means.

5 (F) COMMUNITY CARETAKING EXCEPTION

A reporting party says he has not seen his elderly neighbor for a few days. Newspapers are stacked up, mail hasn't been picked up, dog is barking and the dog dish is empty. Police may force entry to preserve life.

5 (G) VEHICLE INVENTORY EXCEPTION

In accordance with a police agency's policy on vehicle impounds officers may look in containers and trunks in order to make inventory search.
This cannot be done in bad faith as a pretext to a criminal investigation.

A vehicle inventory is done in conjunction with impounding ("seizing") it. Therefore, the decision to impound must be reasonable and appropriate otherwise contraband found during the inventory is tainted.

Officer impounding a vehicle to prevent traffic hazard or risk of damage is reasonable.

*Officer must prove that other viable alternatives were considered before impounding. Officers: How well do you know your department's inventory/impound policy?

5 (H) SCHOOL SEARCHES
School officials may conduct warrantless searches of students if they reasonably believe a violation of law or school policy has occurred or is occurring. Scope of search must be reasonably related to the objectives of the search.

*A *SRO* (School Resource Officer) cannot use or direct school officials as his agent(s) to circumvent his requirement to have probable cause or reasonable suspicion. A SRO can be present when the school conducts an independent search and then act on what was found.

5 (I) FRESH PURSUIT
Police from out of state may pursue into Idaho in fresh pursuit of a fleeing felon.

Idaho officers in fresh pursuit of a felon can pursue and arrest in any territory in the state. The same goes for any crime or traffic offense.

Police may cross territorial limits to assist other officers asking for help.

Police must book suspect in the county he was arrested in.

Idaho law defines "fresh pursuit" more broadly than other states.

IDAHO'S FRESH PURSUIT LAW

19-705 IC. "Fresh pursuit" defined. The term "fresh pursuit" as used in this act shall include fresh pursuit as defined by the common law, and also the pursuit of a person who has committed a felony or who is reasonably suspected of having committed a felony. It shall also include the pursuit of a person suspected of having committed a supposed felony, though no felony has actually been committed, if there is reasonable ground for believing that a felony has been committed. Fresh pursuit as used herein shall not necessarily imply "instant" pursuit, but pursuit without unreasonable delay.

For further clarification consider STATE OF IDAHO v. MATTHEW GILBERT SCOTT Docket No. 37018 -- November 23, 2010

Fresh pursuit thus encompasses: (1) fresh pursuit as defined by the common law; and (2) pursuit of a suspected felon. While I.C. § 19-705 seems to cover only the pursuit of felons, both I.C. §§ 50-209 and 19-701A expand fresh pursuit to traffic infractions.
In determining whether an officer was in fresh pursuit, other jurisdictions look at factors such as:(1) whether the police acted without unnecessary delay; (2) whether the pursuit was continuous and uninterrupted, even if surveillance or knowledge of the suspect's location was interrupted; and (3) whether a close temporal relationship existed between the commission of the offense, the commencement of the pursuit, and the apprehension of the suspect.

Note: While all of the above exceptions do give authority to search without a warrant none of these exceptions stand on their own as sufficient grounds for a warrantless search unless the officer can also show that obtaining a warrant under the circumstances was not practical.

6. ARREST WARRANTS
When can an arrest warrant be served?
- **Felony arrest warrant** may be served <u>anytime day or night</u>.
- **Misdemeanor arrest warrant** may be served day or night if in a public place, but NOT between the hours of 8:00 PM and 08:00 AM at suspect's residence.

If a misdemeanor arrest warrant is authorized for night service or consent is given to enter the residence by a person of authority then police can arrest in the residence at night.

If police have PC to believe the wanted person is in the residence of another they will need a **search warrant** for the body of "Joe Criminal."

STEAGALD v. UNITED STATES, 451 U.S. 204 (1981) U.S. SUPREME COURT
Pursuant to an arrest warrant for one Lyons, Drug Enforcement Administration agents entered petitioner's home to search for Lyons without first obtaining a search warrant. In the course of searching the home, the agents found cocaine and other incriminating evidence, but did not find Lyons. Petitioner was then arrested and indicted on federal drug charges. His pretrial motion to suppress all evidence uncovered during the search of his home on the ground that it was

illegally obtained because the agents had failed to obtain a search warrant was denied by the District Court, and petitioner was convicted. The Court of Appeals affirmed.
Held:
The search in question violated the Fourth Amendment where it took place in the absence of consent or exigent circumstances. Pp. 451 U. S. 211-222.
(a) Absent exigent circumstances or consent, a home may not be searched without a warrant. Two distinct interests were implicated by the search in this case -- Lyons' interest in being free from an unreasonable seizure and petitioner's interest in being free from an unreasonable search of his home. Because the arrest warrant for Lyons addressed only the former interest, the search of petitioner's home was no more reasonable from petitioner's perspective than it would have been if conducted in the absence of any warrant. The search therefore violated the Fourth Amendment. Pp. 451 U. S. 211-216.
(b)
PAYTON v. NEW YORK – 445 U.S. 573 (1980) U.S. SUPREME COURT
These appeals challenge the constitutionality of New York statutes authorizing police officers to enter a private residence without a warrant and with force, if necessary, to make a routine felony arrest. In each of the appeals, police officers, acting with probable cause but without warrants, had gone to the appellant's residence to arrest the appellant on a felony charge and had entered the premises without the consent of any occupant. In each case, the New York trial judge held that the warrantless entry was authorized by New York statutes and refused to suppress evidence that

was seized upon the entry. Treating both cases as involving routine arrests in which there was ample time to obtain a warrant, the New York Court of Appeals, in a single opinion, ultimately affirmed the convictions of both appellants.

Held: *The Fourth Amendment, made applicable to the States by the Fourteenth Amendment, prohibits the police from making a warrantless and nonconsensual entry into a suspect's home in order to make a routine felony arrest. Pp. 445 U. S. 583-603.*

Where can arrest warrants be served?
- In a public place
- At suspect's residence if officer believes he is home
- In the residence of a third party if the person with authority gives police consent to enter
- In the residence of a third party if police have a search warrant for "the body of" the suspect
- Exigent circumstance anywhere

Although officers may forcibly enter to arrest on a misdemeanor /felony <u>arrest warrant</u> we must comply with the knock and announce requirement (barring exigent circumstance).

Note: See page 47 for knock and announce requirement for search warrant service.

**Idaho officers may NOT forcibly enter the residence of a person wanted on an out-of-state felony (extraditable) arrest warrant. Officers can arrest him, but cannot force entry to do so. There are two exceptions:

- Police get a "fugitive to Idaho" warrant
- He flees into the residence

7. SEARCH WARRANTS

Article I section 17 of The Idaho State Constitution mirrors the Fourth Amendment of the U.S. Constitution and protects citizens from unreasonable searches and seizures.

Probable Cause definition #2 (The standard to search): *PC to issue a search warrant is determined by evaluating the totality of circumstances and making a "practical, common-sense decision whether, given all the circumstances set forth in the affidavit before {the magistrate}, including the veracity and 'basis of knowledge' of persons supplying hearsay information, contraband or evidence of a crime will be found in a particular place.*

The Magistrate can rely on hearsay if there is substantial basis to support it. The Magistrate can rely on an anonymous informant if the veracity (reliability and credibility) and basis of knowledge are strong.

An informant's basis of knowledge can be self-verifying given the details provided i.e. a former EOD military man describes bomb making material in someone's garage.

A search warrant must be applied for in the district where the property to be searched is located.

Note: State has jurisdiction on tribal land when crime occurred outside Indian Country.

A search warrant that is not signed by a judge (even accidentally) is NOT valid.

Police must leave a copy of the search warrant and a receipt of things seized behind. An inventory must be made of property taken "in the presence" of person from whom property was taken. In his/her absence the inventory must be filled out in front of one credible witness.

Search Warrants can only be served in the daytime unless authorized for night service on good cause.

Search warrant must be returned within 14 days of issuance. Upon return of the search warrant an affidavit listing the items sized must be included. Once the search warrant is "issued" (signed by the judge) and literally on its way to the address, officers may make entry to secure the residence prior to its arrival.

Police can prevent the suspect from entering his residence without the company/supervision of an officer while search warrant is being issued.

Search warrant may be served electronically to corporations, banks, phone companies and Internet companies.

Pending a search warrant for a vehicle police can seize it.

KNOCK AND ANNOUNCE
The knock and announce requirement exists to prevent property damage and to prevent a violent confrontation with police. *Failure to knock and announce will result in the suppression of evidence. Knock and Announce is implied on a consent entry.

Knock and Announce Exceptions:
- Persons inside are armed
- Evidence may be destroyed
- Suspect may escape
- Persons on premises are engaged in furtive conduct

Without these exceptions a search warrant served without a knock and announce will result in a suppression hearing.
*If the affiant knows the suspects are armed, officers may ask the court for a "no-knock warrant."

The smaller the items being searched for, the broader the scope of the search i.e. looking for photos would include a computer. In this modern world a computer is equivalent to opening a file cabinet drawer.

Police cannot search persons in the residence unless they are specifically named in the warrant. Of course, if police met the Terry pat down requirements they can do a search limited to weapons.

Officers can search the personal effects of overnight guests during the execution of a search warrant.

Every item seized must be supported by PC to believe the items seized are those described in the search warrant.

Plain View: Officer may seize items found outside of the scope of the search warrant if he is where the search warrant authorizes him to be and the item seized is immediately incriminating.

Remember, Plain View Doctrine does not expand the scope of police search. If police think they need broader scope, they should get a second search warrant.

TRACKING DEVICES
The U.S. Supreme Court on 1/23/12 unanimously restricted the police's ability to use a GPS device to track criminal suspects without a search warrant in a first test of how privacy rights will be protected in the digital age. UNITED STATES v. JONES No. 10–1259. Argued November 8, 2011—Decided January 23, 2012 The court rejected the government's view that long-term surveillance of a suspect by GPS tracking is no different than traditional, low-tech forms of monitoring.

ABANDONED PROPERTY
There is no expectation of privacy for abandoned property. Trash placed on curb or edge of property for pick up is okay to take. Same goes for motel wastebasket after guest leaves.

No expectation of privacy from bottle left in interview room by defendant. The DNA sample collected from the bottle is valid.

*If the suspect voluntarily disclaims ownership of an item i.e. a backpack, it can be searched. He voluntarily terminated his interest in property.

END

The following pages are excerpts from my book, RED BADGE.

RED BADGE
A Veteran Peace Officer's Commentary on the Marxist Subversion of American Law Enforcement & Culture

ABOUT THE AUTHOR

Doug Traubel is a thirty-year veteran peace officer. Doug's career began in Chula Vista, California, seven miles from the U.S. – Mexico border. His assignments included patrol officer, field training officer, SWAT team, and Street Team (a proactive patrol unit that targeted gangs and series related crimes IE. robbery and other special enforcement projects).

Doug graduated from The San Diego County Sheriff's Academy in 1986. On the first day of instruction he attended a lecture from Sheriff John Duffy on the history, role and unique authority held by the Constitutional Office of Sheriff. It was then that he developed a reverence for the Office and an understanding of the necessary and substantive differences between Sheriffs, Chiefs of police and federal "law enforcement."

Doug graduated from San Diego State University with a BA in political science (emphasis on constitutional law) and a minor in the Spanish language.

In 1993, Doug was awarded the medal of valor for his response to three hostile, armed men he and his partner confronted while on plain-clothes foot patrol in the alley of a high-crime apartment complex.

Disgusted with the infiltration of Marxist philosophy in the California criminal justice system and its near paralyzing effect on police work, Doug moved to Idaho in 1994. The seed planted by Sheriff John Duffy determined his course: Doug became a Deputy Sheriff. His assignments included patrol, juvenile crimes detective (High School Resource Officer), and gang detective. In 1998, he was awarded the Field Services Director's Award for his work with troubled youth. Doug continues to serve as a trainer and senior criminal investigator.

Doug has been an instructor at the Idaho State Police Academy and an adjunct faculty member at Boise State

University where he taught an upper-division class titled, "Gangs, Drugs and Violence."

The publishing of this book pokes the First Amendment. Is it alive and well? Are we free to speak the truth? Are we free to address taboo topics? Are we free to dissent from the state's narrative?

The level and origin of persecution that this book invokes against the author will prove whether or not the "freedom", "tolerance" and "civil rights" touted by the U.S.A. to its people and the world are lies.

Demonstrating courage with the bold printing of this provocative book, Doug Traubel hopes to inspire courage in YOU to wield the sword of truth and the shield of the First Amendment in defense of America and liberty.

Disclaimer:

The opinions of the author do not reflect or represent those of his employer(s) present or past. This book represents the author's research, personal opinions and thoughts as a private individual and American citizen. And so...

"Agree with me if I seem to you to speak the truth; or, if not, withstand me might and main that I may not deceive you as well as myself in my desire, and like the bee leave my sting in you before I die. And now let us proceed." – Socrates

WARNING!

You are about to read a politically incorrect book; one that will make you feel uncomfortable — as the truth it reveals shatters your paradigm. Sacred cows and taboo topics like race and crime are on the table, not immune here from question or thoughtful scrutiny.

INTRODUCTION

"A nation can survive its fools, and even the ambitious. But it cannot survive treason from within. An enemy at the gates is less formidable, for he is known and carries his banner openly. But the traitor moves amongst those within the gate freely, his sly whispers rustling through all the alleys, heard in the very halls of government itself. For the traitor appears not a traitor; he speaks in accents familiar to his victims, and he wears their face and their arguments, he appeals to the baseness that lies deep in the hearts of all men. He rots the soul of a nation, he works secretly and unknown in the night to undermine the pillars of the city, he infects the body politic so that it can no longer resist. A murderer is less to be feared. The traitor is the plague."– Marcus Tullius Cicero

"Treason doth never prosper, what's the reason? For if it prosper, none dare call it treason."

– Sir John Harrington, 1561-1612

"The individual is handicapped by coming face to face with a conspiracy so monstrous he cannot believe it exists. The American mind simply has not come to a realization of the evil which has been introduced into our midst."
J. Edgar Hoover, Elks magazine, 1956
DOJ-BOI Director, 1924-1935
FBI Director: 1935-1972

Upon walking out the doors at the completion of the U.S. Constitutional Convention a woman asked Benjamin Franklin, "What kind of government did you give us?" He replied, "A Republic, if you can keep it."

The life of our Republic depends on an informed, educated and moral people. It is "We the People" that are to keep our government accountable to the duties and limits placed on it by the U.S. Constitution and its Amendments. But the average American today is ignorant about our government and history; Why? In large part, it is due to the intentional dumbing-down of the population through government controlled public education.

"Give us the child for eight years and it will be a communist forever."   – Vladimir Lenin
(Founder of the Soviet Communist Party)

Oil Magnate and trans-national corporate thug John D. Rockefeller was instrumental in setting up the "General Education Board," forerunner to the U.S. Department of Education. Outwardly presented to the public as an effort to improve education for America's children, its actual long-range strategic goals were three-fold: Orwellian-style thought control, social engineering and the gradual dumbing-down of the nation's youth.

Consider this quote from the General Education Board's Occasional Letter No. 1, issued in 1904: "In our dreams we have limitless resources and the people yield themselves with perfect docility to our molding hands... We have not to raise up from them authors, poets or men of letters...The task we set before ourselves is...to train these people as we find them to a perfectly ideal life just where they are."

Translation: arrest their mental development; form, regiment and control their thoughts, ideas, opinions and expressions; and keep them perpetually placid, as mindless, submissive, obedient servants. Or, as Alexis de Tocqueville forewarned, "...a tyranny of mediocrity, a standardization of mind and spirit and condition."

The corrupting influence of the tax-exempt Rockefeller, Ford and Carnegie Foundations on American education and their overall subversion of American society was so alarming that in 1953 a Congressional Committee headed by Representative Brazilla Carroll Reece of Tennessee attempted to hold a full investigation. Powerful interests in the Nation's Capital ultimately thwarted its efforts (the actual hearings before Congress abruptly ended after only two weeks!).

Rene Wormser was the Reece Committee's general counsel. After the disbandment of the committee, Wormser wrote an expose´ titled, Foundations: Their Power and Influence.

Wormser stated that based on the facts the Reece Committee discovered, "...leads one to the conclusion that there was, indeed, something in the nature of an actual conspiracy among certain leading educators in the United States to bring about Socialism through the use of our school systems..."

In a revealing episode that took place in Autumn of 1953 at the headquarters of the Ford Foundation (after the disbandment of the congressional investigation), Rowan Gaither, who at the time was President of the Ford Foundation, stated to the Reece Committee's Director of Research Norman Dodd:
"Mr. Dodd, all of us here at the policy-making level have had experience, either in OSS or the European Economic Administration, with directives from the White House. We operate under those directives here. Would you like to know what those directives are?"

When Dodd replied in the affirmative, Gaither continued, "The substance of them is that we shall use our grant-making power to so alter life in the United

States that we can be comfortably merged with the Soviet Union."

When Dodd asked Gaither if he would testify to that in front of the Congressional Committee for the record Gaither replied, "This we would not think of doing." (Sources: Alan Stang, Foundations Pay the Way, American Opinion, January 1977 and The Shadows of Power by James Perloff, October 1988).

When one examines the fundamental "altering of American life" and the radical change in the citizen-government relationship financed, crafted and in many ways engineered by tax-exempt foundations over the past 60 years (from something uniquely "American" to something more resembling Eastern European socialism) and then places it in the context of the well-financed Trotskyite "One World Socialist Revolution", the "comfortable merger" begins to crystallize.

Recall that the first communist country in history was an Eastern European dictatorship named the "Union of Soviet SOCIALIST Republics" (U.S.S.R.), more commonly known as the Soviet Union. After seizing power in a bloodthirsty coup, the socialist rulers of the former Russia then went on to mass murder over 60 million of their own citizens and ran the largest network of slave labor camps in history, known as the Gulag, where political prisoners were tortured, starved and worked literally to death. Now, does this sound like the "worker's paradise" that socialists throughout the world proclaimed it was or does it sound more like hell on earth? Is this a system with which you would want to be "comfortably merged" with?

After inflicting its socialist ideology on four generations of Americans, — "Common Core" — is the continuation of this diabolical effort to transform (destroy) America through public "education." Dr. Terrence Moore of Hillsdale College made a compelling argument to that point. He said that through Common Core we are creating, "cultural orphans." In a speech that can be found on You Tube called Story Killers, Moore describes with example after example how Common Core's so-called "rigorous standards aimed at college and career readiness" is rhetoric and not reality.

The 45 states that signed on to Common Core will turn out uneducated worker drones. These drones will have a misunderstanding and negative view of our roots. Students are being raised without knowledge of the depth and context of our rich history. This severs the generational bonds of affection for America. Without affection for America one does not react normally — with jealousy and alarm — when our foundations are attacked. One is merely a spectator on the widget line.

"The greatest evil...is conceived and ordered...in clean, carpeted, warmed and well-lighted offices, by quiet men with white collars and cut fingernails and smooth-shaven cheeks who do not need to raise their voice."
– C.S. Lewis, The Screwtape Letters, (Quoted by President Ronald Reagan before the National Association of Evangelicals, 1983)

In 2008 and again in 2012 America had a choice between two liberal candidates for president and chose Obama, the most far Left. Notwithstanding voter fraud putting him over the top, these elections were the result of generations of "purification" of thought through public education and the media.

"The danger to America is not Barack Obama but a citizenry capable of entrusting a man like him with the Presidency. It will be far easier to limit and undo the follies of an Obama presidency than to restore the necessary common sense and good judgment to a depraved electorate willing to have such a man for their president. The problem is much deeper and far more serious than Mr. Obama, who is a mere symptom of what ails America. Blaming the prince of the fools should not blind anyone to the vast confederacy of fools that made him their prince. The Republic can survive a Barack Obama, who is, after all, merely a fool. It is less likely to survive a multitude of fools such as those who made him their president."

– Anonymous citizen of the Czech Republic

The above quote was sent to me in June of 2009. Within six months of Obama's first term a foreigner saw with great clarity what most here could not.

Imagine what the Czech author believes now after the 2012 election. Granted, Obama's second win was more suspect than his first. In the first election Obama did not win in a single state that has voter ID laws. One-third (16/50) of the states' attorneys general conducted voter fraud investigations and sent them to the U.S. Attorney General, Eric Holder, who did nothing. Prior to Obama, no president had ever won a second term with unemployment over 8%, let alone 15%.

"It is enough that the people know there was an election. The people who cast the votes decide nothing. The people who count the votes decide everything."
– Josef Stalin

Legitimate or not, Obama sat in the Oval Office insulated by the media and supported by large segments of a rapidly changing population made hostile toward our traditions and culture.

Government-controlled "public schools", mainstream media, Hollywood and the courts have indoctrinated and intimidated the majority into processing events through the filter of a false reality developed and financed by powerful and largely "invisible" social engineers. This substitute for truth has impaired our ability to reason and think critically thereby eliminating any effective resistance to the advancement of the Marxist agenda.

Over the last 50 + years — just two generations — Americans have been subjected to the most sophisticated and highly polished propaganda campaign in history; one that would be the envy of North Korea, Red China, or the Soviet Union.

Today, voters truly believe they have two opposing ideologies from which to choose at the polls in national elections. What they really have in the two establishment political parties are nothing more than what Judge Andrew Napolitano has correctly described as "two wings of the same bird of prey", that 'bird' being a predatory government lurching over the American people, devouring our rights and our property piece by piece.

It is always the so-called "Right" that compromises. The Left never gives up ground. This is how over two generations we moved incrementally toward socialism. The GOP is merely the controlled (false) opposition. Former presidential candidate and Reagan Administration official Alan Keyes has described the sham that is our national "elections" as the equivalent of playing in a rigged casino — "The House" always wins — to your great detriment!
(Note: For elaboration on the mechanisms of propaganda and the false choice of candidates and political parties, see the Chapter Eleven of this book).

At no other time in U.S. history could the nebulous slogan "change" have moved the majority (ostensibly) to vote for a candidate. Burdened with guilt spun by Marxists over what they describe as America's original sin (slavery) and its vestiges, white voters treated their ballots like antidepressants. What should have been a footnote in history — Obama's race — became the obsession of his supporters, the focus of the media and a shield from criticism and accountability.

By voting for symbolism (race) over substance, voters did something more profound than electing America's first "black" (mulatto) president: they unwittingly elected a vehemently anti-American president.

Packaged by a complicit media as the savior, buyer's remorse set in as Obama defined "change" for the country one disastrous decision at a time — intentionally destroying the economy, our stature in the world, our institutions, and our culture.

Over the last 20 years, there has been an unrelenting effort by Marxists to soften the minds of American voters to embrace "change." Change from what? Change from a fictitious crisis of oppression, hate and intolerance perpetrated by white males and Christians.

An anti-American, psychological rip current is pulling our culture and institutions to the Left. Born of disinformation, revisionist history, ignorance, intimidation and moral relativism — as many as half of Americans citizens are increasingly becoming either indifferent about defending tradition or hostile toward it.

Marxists masquerade as champions of factions they deem "victims." They pit the victims against the vilified majority and rally them to attack our institutions and traditions as instruments of oppression. Arguing against the narrative paints one a hater. Consequently, the majority's timidity and silence encourage and embolden its enemies rendering the anchor points of America's culture and institutions defenseless.

America's two dominant political parties have become indistinguishable; they offer no hope for a restoration of America's traditions, unique culture and greatness. Each is trying to promote itself as the party of inclusion: they want to be all things to all people – except of course to the vilified, traditional White Christian majority.

Neither the Republicans nor the Democrats speak as though they want to really lead the country and promote the betterment of our peoples' standard of living – they seek only to manage and oversee its squabbling factions while maintaining their privileged, regal lifestyle. They have no desire to be our saviors or the saviors of our country – they want to remain our "Overlords."

These parties are not motivated by the paramount objective of preserving the constitutional and cultural integrity of our nation. Maintaining and solidifying power is their only objective.

The Reform Party, Libertarian Party, Constitution Party, Populist Party, and others were excluded from the 2000, 2004, 2008, 2012 and 2016 presidential debates. The mainstream media give little coverage to these increasingly popular parties, making obvious its complicit role in insulating and protecting the "two-party oligarchy."

(For those who insist a two-party "system" is adequate and acceptable, remember that a two-party system is only one more than dictatorship. And think about how much easier it is for two parties to collude and collaborate against the interests of the American people than it would be for four, five or more parties to do so in a truly "open field" of candidates and choices).

Most Republican congressmen have been intimidated or indoctrinated by the same thought control as the public. In addition, professional lobbyists and pressure groups buy, intimidate or blackmail our representatives. This is why we see compromise after compromise by so-called conservatives. This is why we see only political theater and no accountability for scandal after scandal.

In reality, until the unforeseen arrival of President Trump we were living under a one-party system. At the national level, the Republican Party has merely been the "controlled opposition" — a sham opposition — a political charade. Its inaction is surrender. Under Obama both houses of Congress had Republican majorities (247 in the House and 54 in the Senate). There has not been this many Republicans in Congress since the Civil War and yet with that majority they do not hold Obama accountable or even put him in check.

An example of this is the House and Senate on 12/18/15 passing a $1.1 Trillion omnibus spending bill. The 1,582-page bill funded Obama's Syrian-Muslim refugee plan, Climate Control agenda, Obama Care and Planned Parenthood. The GOP's disdain for Donald Trump was driven by fear that this outsider would expose the truth, strip power from the establishment and work to restore the Republic, returning power to The People.

Hillary Clinton was to be Obama's third term. Prior to the Trump phenomena America was in the final two years of complete transformation into an authoritarian, Soviet-style police state. With the increasing takeovers of local police departments by the federal government (through Department of Justice "monitors" and "consent decrees"), the passage of Obamacare, and the National Defense Authorization Act of 2012 (NDAA) — which guts your constitutional rights and essentially nullifies the U.S. Bill of Rights — there was no end in sight to the Obama Administration's usurpation and unconstitutional power grabs. Whether President Trump will be merely a speed bump to the

Left or a pivot point to the restoration of the Republic is yet to be seen.

Can one man undo over 85 years of Marxist social engineering, public indoctrination, judicial activism, socialism, and dilution of our culture through colonization, welfare dependence and a web of lurching unconstitutional bureaucracy? He interrupted the Left's momentum, but it is not defeated. The Deep State and most of the media conspire to discredit and stop him.

International communists are backing what the American media casually call "protesters." These are highly organized, planned events. Thousands of people, many from out of the area, do not appear spontaneously and even at the same locations in different cities. Not only are these violent people not protesters, but neither are they rioters. They are worse. They are agents of communist revolution funded by foreign powers.

President Trump's oath is to defend the USA from all enemies — foreign and domestic. Follow the money. Antifa and Black Lives Matter are supported by our enemies. President Trump must use all of his presidential power and resources to defend the USA from these domestic communist revolutionaries. This is of course made extremely difficult when "news" networks confuse the people by making the revolutionary look righteous.

Roger Stone was correct when he said of CNN, it "...is not a news organization. It is a radical propaganda arm of the Soros Corporation."

Zbigniew Brzezinski, former National Security Advisor to President Jimmy Carter, Executive Director of the Trilateral Commission, member of the Board of Directors of the Council on Foreign Relations, Columbia University professor, Director of the Research Institute on International Change, avowed Marxist and one of the primary behind-the-scenes puppet masters of Barack Hussein Obama, wrote the following in his revealing, but little –known 1976 book, Between Two Ages:

"The nation-state is gradually yielding its sovereignty... Further progress will require greater American sacrifices. More intensive efforts to shape a new world monetary structure will have to be undertaken, with some consequent risk to the present relatively favorable American position."

(Think of our government's unwillingness to defend our borders, the move toward a borderless "North American Union", our military forces increasingly fighting under United Nations command and control, the destruction of the American dollar, the massive reduction in our standard of living coupled with the simultaneous increased costs, and the world-wide monetary chaos and calls for a "one world currency.")

Brzezinski continues:

"The (coming) era involves the gradual appearance of a more controlled society. Such a society would be dominated by an elite, unrestrained by traditional values. Soon it will be possible to assert almost continuous surveillance over every citizen and maintain up-to-date complete files containing even the most personal information about the citizen. These files will be subject to instantaneous retrieval by the authorities."

Think of our corrupt, out-of-control, no accountability federal government and the recent scandals and revelations regarding the truly Orwellian surveillance, spying and eavesdropping capabilities of the U.S. National Security Agency. Parts of our government spied on presidential candidate Donald Trump. Once elected a fabricated dossier – paid for by the Clinton Foundation and the DNC – was sworn to be true before a FISA court judge (multiple times) to authorize an investigation of our duly elected President. It does not matter if you like or dislike Donald Trump.

Due Process and Rule of Law are nonpartisan pillars of the Republic and must be defended. Acts of treason and sedition must be brought to account – through military courts if necessary.

Brzezinski, the proud Marxist and high-level government advisor: "Marxism represents a further vital and creative stage in the maturing of man's universal vision ... Marxism is simultaneously a victory of the external, active man over the inner, passive man and a victory of reason over belief ... Marxism, disseminated on the popular level in the form of communism, represents a major advance in man's ability to conceptualize his relationship to the world." And this man was influencing President Obama and shaping government policies that dramatically affect your future, your country, your individual freedoms, and your American way of life!

Socialism and Communism come from the same seed — Marxism. The differences are only a matter of the degree of authoritarian or totalitarian centralized governmental control over the means of production, the population and the distribution of goods and services.

By using what the "Frankfurt School" Marxists dubbed "critical theory", 21st Century Neo-Marxists get a foothold in societies first by finding fault, then identifying injured parties, and finally by organizing them in opposition to the institutions and establishment they seek to overthrow. The simplicity of this is that one can find fault in literally anything. And so it is with Marxists when they look at America.

The United States of America is the greatest country in world history. Yet Marxists always find fault and say, "There is much more work to do..." as if great flaws still exist and "change" is the aim of their struggle. Their protests are never based on righteousness or principle, only power and control. They do not truly care about those whose grievances they claim to champion. They appeal to their power base with emotion. The architects know it is a fraud, but the dupes, knaves and followers swallow the clichés and propaganda time and again, and regurgitate it ad nauseam. Marxist leaders posture to do the impossible. They promise to perfect society as envisioned in their populist, naive ideology.

The true goal is the seizure of power through subversion for the benefit of an elite ruling class. To accomplish this America must be discredited in the eyes of the majority. To that end, the Diversity Movement promotes the myth that even with a "black" president in the White House put there by white votes — the U.S. is a racist, bigoted country with no moral authority that oppresses victim classes made of non-white minorities, women and homosexual/transgender people. This hate and intolerance is said to come from generations of political and cultural dominance by white male conservatives and Christians.

None of these supposed victim groups of "white oppression" truly improve their circumstance under democrat-Marxist policies, but rather they become dependent on government programs translating to votes for democrat politicians. Ben Shapiro hit the mark when he said, for a Marxist "...everyone is either a tool or an obstacle."

Marxists care only about the revolution, not the person and not the issue. In contrast, under Trump's free market and US sovereignty policies we have the lowest unemployment ever for blacks and Hispanics and the lowest unemployment in 18 years for women. The booming economy is not the result of Obama's Marxist policies. That is a baseless claim of the Left desperate to be seen as credible. Kanye West has seen through the deception of the Left and boldly educates other black Americans to leave the government plantation.

Marxists disparage traditionalists. In order to discredit their adversaries, they dismiss with laughter being pinned with the labels, "Marxist" and "Socialist" as though it is crazy talk coming from backward thinking people. Obama said of his critics, "They get bitter, they cling to guns or religion or antipathy to people who aren't like them or anti-immigrant sentiment or anti-trade sentiment as a way to explain their frustration." Regardless of the refusal of Marxist ideologues like Obama to wear their brand openly, their transparent agenda and template convicts them just the same.

Marxism is the absolute consolidation of power and the expansion of regulation and control over individuals, capital, private property and businesses. Public dependence on government services reduces resistance to its unconstitutional overreach. What it cannot seduce it forces to conform. Marxism's enormous infrastructure is led by self-serving, self-righteous, secular and self-anointed elite.

Marxism is a philosophy that uses the worst of human nature to enslave the best of human nature. It is a lie and a threat to man's God-given, unalienable rights.

Winston Churchill put it best: "Socialism is a philosophy of failure, the creed of ignorance, and gospel of envy; its inherent virtue is the equal sharing of misery."

In order to see the modern face of Marxism in the United States, the reader must look through two lenses: The Diversity Movement and Political Correctness.

The Diversity Movement is Marxism repackaged with a benevolent mask. It is a highly coordinated and well-financed effort among self-validating and overlapping forces; each promoting varying radical forms of "social justice" as the remedy for the BIG LIE about the character and history of the United States.

The premise of the BIG LIE is that our history (and most of world history) is nothing more than a series of injustices by whites resulting in oppression and the inequitable distribution of wealth, power, access, privilege and capital.

The Diversity Movement controls most of America's Academia Class. Its ranks comprise the overwhelming majority of instructors in public schools and universities. The Academia Class in concert with most of the media, Hollywood and activist judges promote the Big Lie.

There is just enough truth woven in their lie (much of it out of context) to sound credible to a publicly "educated" population; one with shallow knowledge, short memories, shorter attention spans and weak in critical thinking. The Left amplify and validate each other. For over four generations they have worked successfully to shape public opinion.

Classic Marxism pits the labor class against those who control the means of production (proletariat vs. the bourgeoisie). Today's Marxism pits balkanized camps, deemed disenfranchised "victims," against what they are taught is their common oppressor — the Old Guard culture (made up mostly of Christians and conservative whites).

The Diversity Movement's aim is the forced realignment of society. Right out of Orwell's 1984, the Diversity Movement uses the thought-limiting language of "Newspeak" to champion unobjectionable-sounding causes like diversity, inclusion, tolerance, equality and justice. How can anyone be opposed to these ideals?

Marxist social engineers are wordsmiths. These terms have been inverted. They have radical, culturally suicidal definitions for America. They contradict our history, ethos, and Judeo-Christian cultural roots.

We need to relearn how to think critically in order to see the deception. Walk with me through this mental exercise: Ask yourself, "How do contradictions hold up in the natural world?" A molecule of H_2O can be liquid, solid or gas. Each has its own name because each has

distinct qualities. If something called by a name does not reflect the unique characteristics expected of it there is a deception, a contradiction, a lie.
Calling steam "water" does not transfer the defining properties of water and allow me to pour steam into a bucket. Water is water. Steam is steam. Ice is ice. Marriage is marriage. Words mean things.

The danger in bending, contorting and misusing words and obfuscating their meaning was recognized over 2,500 years ago when the famous Chinese philosopher and teacher Confucius admonished his fellow Chinamen by telling them to "call a spade a spade" (Confucius meant that literally).

Just as two objects in the material world cannot occupy the same space at the same time, we cannot permit contradictions to occupy the same space in our mind. Doing otherwise creates confusion; it arrests the reasoning ability needed to recognize deception and defend truth.

The Diversity Movement's premise is a deception. Its architects seek to vilify, discredit, debase and dispossess the culture that built this great nation. They preach tolerance, but are intolerant of our nation's heritage and the race and religion of those who built it (White Christians).

Their aim is to sever any remaining ties that this generation has with our roots. Their objective is a forced redistribution of power and wealth. To accomplish this, they must subvert and transform our culture and institutions. This is done by intimidating and shunning tradition while ushering in a rapidly forming new majority made of a permanent, unassimilated underclass to support them.

Political Correctness is the hammer of the Diversity Movement. It is found on campus — where grades suffer when you are treated as a heretic for challenging the state narrative; at work — when you are snared by a double standard hostile workplace complaint; on the street — when you are selectively charged with a hate crime; in civil court — when your business settles a bogus discrimination suit by hateful anti-White, anti-Christian, shake-down artists; and in the media — convicting and shunning you as a "racist" or bigot in the court of public opinion for speaking outside of the "correct" parameters.

Most of all it is in you. Political Correctness is a self-policing force of intellectual paralysis brought about by the conditioning (purifying or washing) of our minds to dodge the consequences of dissent by either being silent or parroting the false narrative. This conditioning of passivity to the Big Lie is the product of the complicit media, Marxist "educators", liberal human resource administrators, corrupt court officials, so-called civil rights activists, and leftist Hollywood — all promoting and legitimizing the false narrative and casting the roles of victims and suspect.

Political Correctness disarms tradition. It creates an environment of diluted discourse, censorship and self-censorship. Through intimidation, it enforces conformity of thought and expression that subvert our heroes and founding ethos.

A clear example of how political correctness is advanced is a new word: Micro-aggression. This is a Marxist construct that means: "Social exchanges in which a member of a dominant culture says or does something, often accidentally, and without intended malice, that belittles and alienates a member of a marginalized group." There are seminars based on Columbia University Psychology Professor Derald Wing Sue's book, Microaggressions in Everyday Life: Race, Gender and Sexual Orientation. This is an effort to cultivate hypersensitivity of "victim" groups and intimidate the legitimate and traditional American society to silence.

The First Amendment was given to us by the anti-federalists precisely to protect (unpopular) political speech, but for many whom think outside the confines of the state narrative they are too intimidated to use it. They see reputations destroyed by the media for defending traditional values and violent attacks for simply wearing a MAGA ball cap. Tradition loses ground without a voice and a fight.

For more evidence of the indoctrination by political correctness in education read 48 Liberal Lies about American History (That you Probably Learned in School) by Professor Larry Schweikart. You will see the marginalization of our Founding Fathers and missing facts that mislead students about the history and character of America.

Have you scrolled through a calendar lately? We no longer celebrate George Washington's birthday, the victorious military leader of the War of Independence and our Nation's first president. As a poor substitute we have "Presidents' Day" which fails to honor Washington's actual birthday and minimizes him from the national memory.

Martin Luther King Jr. has his own day. Rather than consolidate civil rights leaders and call it "Civil Rights Day" MLK gets his own day, but not the father of our country, George Washington. Why?

MLK's face and name are used as propaganda to market social justice. This is a man that said and did some admirable things no doubt, and whose FBI file remains sealed because what is in there likely proves rumors that would discredit his lionization and be unproductive to the Left.

Specifically, there have long been rumors of MLK committing brutal "date rapes" of white women in his hotel rooms and cavorting with communists. The closest we get to the texture of the content in the file is a recorded interview of Jackie Kennedy where she calls MLK "terrible," "a phony" and "tricky." This is someone who would have heard regular and candid conversations about the FBI's surveillance of MLK spoken between the president and his brother the U.S. Attorney General. It has been fifty years and the MLK file remains closed. This is Soviet-style suppression of information.

Then there are Earth Day, Cinco de Mayo, Native American Day, United Nations Day, Ramadan and Kwanzaa. Each of these squares on the calendar is a launch pad for Marxists to bash America and build momentum year after year. Black people have an entire month to prop up their victim status (albeit the shortest month of the year — clearly a racist conspiracy). The end of the calendar closes with public schools inviting families to a "winter festival" concert. Saying, "Merry Christmas" is presumptuous and offensive (a "micro-aggression").

Conspicuously absent of mention in the U.S. Press, is a story run in the United Kingdom's Daily Mail on December 16, 2015 about Riverheads High School in Virginia where in a 9th grade "calligraphy lesson" students were required to write the opening of the shahada, the Muslim conversion prayer: "There is no god but Allah, and Muhammad is the messenger of Allah." Meanwhile, in Johnson County, Kentucky the Board of Education forced the production of Charlie Brown's Christmas to remove Biblical reference to the Gospel of Luke.

Marxists want to remove Christmas as a national holiday. It is part of its agenda to secularize the population. Already, they have created an environment where it takes some courage to utter the words,

"Merry Christmas" and doing so instantly creates tension in any room. "Happy Holidays" is a safe alternative that we are sold as inclusive. In fact it is exclusive. It excludes the name of our national holiday.

Marxists divide. They are desperate to find and create opportunities to defend counter cultures and express selective outrage over tradition. They advance the Cultural Revolution by making issues out of non-issues like the names and mascots of long-standing sports teams and landmarks. They pounce on any opportunity to stoke emotion, fear and division.

In the wake of the sensationalized reporting of a lone, Confederate-flag-wearing nut's murderous attack on parishioners at the Emanuel African Methodist Episcopal Church in Charleston, South Carolina (June 18, 2015) — where nine people were killed, New Orleans Mayor Mitch Landrieu swayed the City Council to vote to remove Civil War monuments including that of General Robert E. Lee (erected in 1884) from prominent places. He described the move as a "courageous decision to turn a page on our divisive past and chart the course for a more inclusive future." Not to be outdone, on July 7, 2015 the Memphis City Council voted unanimously to exhume the body of Confederate General Nathan Bedford Forrest and move it as if the soil is contaminated. This is political fanaticism.

The Confederate flag is coming down from government buildings throughout the south as if it is a symbol of hate not heritage. These self-righteous, irrational and fanatical acts by state and local governments are out of proportion to current events, void of historical perspective and fuel the Big Lie. Riding the wave of emotion and spin the PC police kick American tradition and heritage to the curb.

There is no room at the table for America. Americans are in retreat from their own government.

I will have none of that! I refuse to suspend reality! I will not abandon our history, heroes and heritage! I did not take an oath to defend a lie! It is time to wield the sword of truth and go on the offense to fight for what is left of America! That is what Red Badge does and prepares you to do.

The U.S. is the greatest country in the history of humankind. No country — but America — has had as large and broad a spectrum of its citizens (regardless of race or sex) enjoy such a high average standard of living with almost limitless social mobility. It is the free market and limits placed on government that unleashed the competition of ideas and rewards that rivaled or surpassed the world in every field. Americans walked on the moon; our flag is there! We lead the way. We are the most philanthropic nation in the world. America is exceptional!

Sit back for a moment and think of the countless masses of downtrodden and oppressed from the Third World who have risked their lives by boarding small boats and homemade rafts, braved 100-foot crushing waves and shark-filled oceans on the chance that they'll make it to our shores and have a shot at the "American Dream!"

The American experience has proven that a free market economy and a constitutional republic is the most moral and productive framework for man. The free market most closely mirrors man in his natural state where he created, competed, bartered, overcame adversity, and improved his skill sets. The rule of law protected the individual from mob rule.

Our example of limited government and freedom became a beacon to the world. It caused a brain drain on other countries as the best and brightest immigrated, assimilated and created. Our history is proof that the human spirit thrives best with freedom, private property rights, individual responsibility, small government and self-reliance. Today, Marxism has Lady Liberty in a headlock and its hand in her purse.

Political Correctness has rendered us nearly defenseless to our dispossession. With the American mind intimidated — the Diversity Movement vilifies tradition and promotes cultural anarchy virtually unopposed. Our roots to liberty and moral absolutes have grown shallow in the shadow of intimidation and in the soil of ignorance.

America's Old Guard culture and heritage are being demonized, debased and rejected. Hating our roots, heritage, language and history is the new patriotism. A cultural vacuum is being formed.

Society persecutes anyone who refutes the purported ethos of the Diversity Movement (tolerance, acceptance, diversity). If you are a realist you are a racist.

Fear of persecution results in a passive majority. At the same time architects of the Marxist revolution raise their volume, promoting the Big Lie and quickening their cadence daily, marching unopposed toward the goal of a highly regulated society to bring order and fill the vacuum they create.

The promotion of (radical) diversity as the remedy for the false crisis of hate and bigotry has divided America and turned us against our heritage. Our identity is unraveling. No longer are there moral or cultural absolutes. Marxists have smashed our compass with the heel of their jackboot.

So-called tolerance is the state religion. It has become the opiate of the masses. Judgment and condemnation have been suspended; except for America's Puritan, Anglo-Saxon, Christian roots. Tradition falls outside of the state's protection. With that deliberate exception, Marxists make all cultures and lifestyles feel welcome and equal — for now. In the end, there will be a culling. The least productive segments of society together with the most threatening to the regime (its most ardent, organized supporters) will be eliminated.

Marxists need the police to embrace their agenda in order to complete and secure the transfer of power. Police must be depended on for crushing counter-revolutionary and post-revolutionary rebellion. Just as successive generations of children were programmed to accept, parrot and obey the Big Lie, so too have generations of peace officers. They feel noble in their ignorance.

RED BADGE will spur discussion on the importance of an officer's oath, local police control, and a citizen's role in a criminal justice system under intense federal pressure to conform to its rapidly expanding Marxist agenda.

CHAPTER THREE
The Purpose Of Government

If you have ever felt small in the shadow of bureaucracy perhaps you asked, "What is the purpose of government?"

The answer is found in one of the four "organic laws" of the United States all of which are codified (law) found in Volume 18 of the Revised Statutes of the United States. Enacted by the 43rd Congress (A.D. 1873-1875) and published by the Government Printing Office in A.D. 1878); it is known as – The Declaration of Independence.

The Declaration is more than an historical document; it is law. It spells out for us binding fundamental truths that define the context and perspective of our nation at inception and the corresponding fundamental purpose of the Republic that emerged.

The document declares: "We hold these truths to be self-evident..." Self-evident means that what follows (the truths) are not to be subjected to debate or further examination: "...that all men are created..." This means that there is an architect and we are His creation: "...equal and are endowed by – their creator – with certain unalienable Rights..." This means that man did not give us our rights, but God did. Therefore, these rights cannot be separated from us: "...to secure these rights, governments are instituted among men ..."

So we see here the purpose of government. It is not to make sure you wear your seat belt or to protect you from obesity by banning big gulps. The Declaration tells us the purpose of government is to secure God-given rights. Whether or not you are a believer in God is irrelevant; this is part of the ethos that distinguishes us as "Americans."

"You have rights antecedent to all earthly governments; rights that cannot be repealed or restrained by human laws; rights derived from the Great Legislator of the Universe." John Adams

Attorney and 2004 presidential candidate, Michael Peroutka, of The Institute on the Constitution calls this historical and legal perspective, "The American View." He acknowledges that we, "...do not live there now."

If we are to restore our Republic, we must center up on The American View again or else surrender to the final transformation of moral relativism and state worship.

In a healthy country, it would be inconsequential how vigorously atheists rail against The American View. The only matter of relevance to an atheist's position on the purpose of government is his unalienable right to voice his wrong opinion (as measured by the law).

Our founders told us that our republic depends on a virtuous and educated people. Without an agreed fixed standard to measure by we find ourselves adrift and rotting from within. We need a restoration. This cannot be done in the cultural vacuum of moral relativism promoted by the architects of the intolerant diversity movement that has rendered us rudderless and self-destructive.

Despite what you might have been taught in public school or heard in the media, "separation of church and state" is not in the Constitution. That phrase comes from a letter penned by Thomas Jefferson to the Danbury Baptist Church. What the First Amendment of the Bill of Rights does say is, "Congress shall make no law respecting an establishment of religion, or prohibiting the free exercise thereof..."

The Constitution protects us from a theocracy; NOT from the moral compass of Christianity. The repeated and out of context references to Jefferson's "separation of church and state" rather than Madison's Constitution has confused us.

It was absurd for President Barack Hussein Obama to suggest we are no more a Christian nation than we are a nation of any other faith(s). While the blood spilled by others of different faiths for America is no less real or appreciated, in the balance the crosses in Arlington National Cemetery say it all.

Furthermore, our federal buildings are replete with Biblical references – including the Supreme Court. Look up photo journalist Carrie Devorah's, "God in the Temple of Government" for a snapshot of just some of the evidence. Even though CSPAN, CNN, MSNBC, FOX et al. crop out these Bible inspired images when filming the Capitol or Supreme Court, these bold monuments stand to the naked eye as a testament from our forebears about the inextricable Christian values (mortar) that are the root of our legal and cultural compass. Christian or not, in these times of deception and confusion we must center up on The American View to find clarity about who we are, what we stand for and where we are headed.

We must recognize that when laws conflict with the limits of the U.S. Constitution (the supreme fixed standard) they are usurpations. "...and deserve to be treated as such." — (Alexander Hamilton)
While these usurpations may look like law and are treated as law by "law enforcement" and the courts, they are what the Declaration of Independence describes as, "pretended legislation" or put another

way: illegitimate. Case law, executive orders and regulatory violations are examples of this; Congress did not pass them so they cannot be law.

The proper role of the Supreme Court is to measure law NOT interpret it or make it. They are to hold the ruler: the fixed standard of the Constitution — to what Congress passes and the President signs.

In its proper and intended role, the Supreme Court would ensure that the Constitution protects us from our best intentions. The Supreme Court's purpose is to defend the Constitution not to treat it as a "living (morphing) document." But, instead it rubber stamps political agendas and makes what lawyers have come to call, "case law." Case law is a misnomer because again — only Congress has the authority to make law. What the court is empowered to do is render rulings; in other words, "measure the law" and rule it constitutional or unconstitutional.

In instances where the Supreme Court settles disputes between states, their ruling is only binding to the parties in the dispute; otherwise they would be "making law" and violating the separation of powers. The Supreme Court is not empowered by the Constitution to interpret the law, only to measure it.

Interpreting law places the Supreme Court as law maker; a constitutional role reserved for Congress exclusively. Not only can the Supreme Court not make law, neither can the President do so unilaterally. Executive orders are NOT law. Although they look like law, they are to apply only to employees of the executive branch and on areas of exclusive federal control like post offices and military bases.

Written in simple language our Constitution makes all of this clear. What turned us on our head is when the Supreme Court acted unconstitutionally and gave itself the (illegitimate) power of judicial review in Marbury vs. Madison. This case made the Supreme Court the law of the land rather than the Constitution.

The unchallenged and unconstitutional practice of judicial review creates volumes of "case law."

Generations of case law argued by lawyers trained in that faulty reasoning takes us more often than not farther away from the fixed standards of the organic law found primarily in the U.S. Constitution and the Declaration of Independence.

Essential to the restoration of the Republic is The People embracing the fixed standards underpinning our legal and cultural foundation. Through this, we can stop further devolution into the subjective, sometimes arbitrary and always prejudicial mire of social justice over criminal justice.

Why is the restoration of the fixed standards important? Think of builders. In ancient days, the fixed standard of measurement was a cubit — the length of the king's forearm, from the elbow to the tip of the middle finger. Over time a more precise fixed standard evolved — the ruler.

A builder who receives blue prints cannot know how to interpret the intent of the architect without a "fixed standard" of measurement to guide him on the intended dimensions of the design. Our fixed standards of governance (the organic law) have been usurped by the whims of special interests and an occupation government that Professor Edward Erle of UC San Bernardino describes as, an Administrative State. This he says is a system where administration and regulation replace politics as the ordinary means of making policy. The Administrative State elevates the welfare of the collective over the rights and liberties of the individual.

The Administrative State has been superimposed over the Constitution; both are visible, but the former has taken over. The Administrative State was built incrementally by the misuse of the Commerce Clause; it is an occupation government. We still see the three branches of government, but it is theater.

Another essential component to restoring the Republic is that peace officers remain accountable locally and that they understand their duty (by oath) to interpose themselves between The People whose rights they protect and pretended legislation; much of it from the aforementioned Administrative State (occupation government). The Office of Sheriff is uniquely designed for this purpose.

Interposition stems from Article VI that requires all public officials to take an oath to "...uphold the United States Constitution." Therefore, it is possible for a peace officer to refuse to enforce "a law" and not be breaking the law by committing perjury (violating his oath) but, in fact, upholding the law. In this instance, his disobedience is obedience (to his constitutionally required oath). Ideally, there would be a moral and educated people in the jury who stand to nullify the charge against him.

Consider the historic Rosa Parks case. Forget that this poor, hardworking seamstress was secretary of the local NAACP and an activist who in 1955, 1956 and 1957 attended summer training sessions at the Highlander Folk School in Mount Eagle, Tennessee. The "school" was founded by James Dombrowski and Myles Horton, both members of the Communist Party (MLK was a fellow student). While her refusal to give up her seat was most likely a scripted event tied to an agenda, she was morally correct to defy state law based on Plessy v. Ferguson (separate but equal). Plessy v. Ferguson was erroneously treated as the "law" of the land. This "case law" was pretended legislation. It was produced by the Supreme Court, not Congress; therefore, it was not and could not be law. Article I, Section 1 of the U.S. Constitution says that "all" legislative powers shall be vested in Congress. How much does that leave for the other two branches? Answer: None.

If the responding peace officer stood on his oath and simply refused to enforce immoral and pretended legislation Rosa would not have been arrested for disturbing the peace; she did nothing wrong. This is an example of interposition.

Interposition should have been applied to the enforcement of gun seizures in the aftermath of Hurricane Katrina when federal and local authorities unconstitutionally seized law abiding citizens' weapons. The Sheriff should have stopped the feds and prohibited the local agencies from powering up with them.

The Role of Sheriff

The Sheriff is the only elected peace officer in the country. He answers to his boss: The People; not to judges, not to the president, not to the governor. In most states, it is a constitutional office.

The Sheriff is The Peoples' guardian. The 2014 spectacle on Cliven Bundy's ranch in Clark County, Nevada is an example of what happens when there is a weak Sheriff in office. It should have been through the advocacy and authority of the Office of Sheriff and then the State Attorney General, that Bundy's original grievance was vetted and argued. The Sheriff's late entry on stage caused Bundy's argument to be unclear to the nation. This resulted in a motley band of protesters arriving — most fueled by noble intentions — with a minority in the mix looking for a flash point to a revolution.

A Constitutional Sheriff on the front line with the facts at his side could have brought about a victory for liberty. The Sheriff's absence not only contributed to chaos and confusion, but allowed the unconstitutional Bureau of Land Management to overreact unchecked with grossly disproportionate, unnecessary and illegitimate force against The People.

If I was a Sheriff my mission statement would read something like this:

The Sheriff and his deputies will honor their oath to defend the U.S. Constitution and the State Constitution through keeping inviolate the solemn role of Sheriff as the Chief Law Enforcement Officer of the County and The Peoples' Guardian; by protecting the residents of the County from criminals of all stripes – including agents of an overreaching state or federal government; preserving the peace with grace, mercy and moral agency; and at the same time being courageous in the face of danger as we demonstrate the humble heart of a servant and the protective instincts of a warrior.

The Role of the Citizen

While the Sheriff has a role to interpose, the citizen has a role too. Citizens must understand their authority to nullify (render impotent) pretended legislation and the misapplication of law. Both interposition and nullification are powers that come from the Constitution and Bill of Rights.

Nullification is a right of The People under the 9th Amendment albeit not expressly stated. It is an "unenumerated" right that can be applied to law and pretended legislation. The Supreme Court implicitly recognized The People's right to nullify in Sparf v. United States (1895). The court noted that judges have no recourse if a jury acquits a defendant even when done in the face of overwhelming evidence of guilt. Since the Sparf decision, the Supreme Court has taken the opposite view.

BLACK'S LAW DICTIONARY (2009) defines *Nullification* as: "A jury's knowing and deliberate rejection of the evidence or refusal to apply the law either because the jury wants to send a message about some social issue that is larger than the case itself or because the result dictated by law is contrary to the jury's sense of justice, morality, or fairness."

Federal and State governments do not want citizens to know about their authority to nullify because it places power where it rightly belongs: in the hands of The People where it could challenge what has to a large extent become a for-profit, self-serving, power hungry court system and government.

Certainly nullification is a problem in the hands of an uneducated and immoral people for example in places like the Bronx borough of New York City where Bronx Juries are common. The term refers to a mostly minority jury that refuses to convict minority defendants even when evidence of guilt is overwhelming. Bronx juries can be found in other cities with large minority populations like Baltimore, Maryland.

In Baltimore it is often difficult for black jurors to deliberate a guilty verdict on black defendants as a result of intimidation ("stitches for snitches"), shared gang affiliation, racial loyalty, or out of some odd notion of reckoning shaped by social justice. This brand of Bronx-nullification is not legitimate because its genesis is immorality, but the effect is the same: acquittal. Interestingly, Maryland's constitution recognizes jury nullification in Article 23.

Professor Paul Butler of Georgetown University encourages the misuse of jury nullification by blacks as a tool to fight against (his perception of) a racist criminal justice system. In his essay, "Racially Based Jury Nullification: Black Power in the Criminal Justice System" he argues that race can be an appropriate factor legally and morally for jurors to consider when deliberating a guilty verdict. He urges black jurors to be conscious of the political power of nullification, "...in the interest of the black community."

Nullification is distinguished from a mistake by jurors. It requires subjective intent. The most well-known example of the down side of nullification is the O.J. Simpson double murder case. The jury's subjective intent was race-based, arguably to send a political message to white America protesting what they perceive to be rampant police misconduct and disproportional incarceration of black men. These destructive brands of nullification will become more common as the population becomes more Balkanized.

A contrasting example of a proper use of nullification is a case in Detroit, Michigan. Neighbors turned vigilantes and set fire to a crack house. The two defendants confessed to the crime of arson. Their actions followed the transformation of a once peaceful neighborhood where because of the crack house kids could no longer play outside. Police were ineffective, but arson ended the problem. The social condition and the failed attempts by the system to address the chronic and dangerous problem brought sympathy from the jury. They used their moral agency and nullified what they weighed as noble-cause crime.

An example of government's misuse of nullification is sanctuary cities for illegal aliens. This practice of local governments nullifying immigration law is not consistent with the fixed standards because border protection is an expressed constitutional duty assigned to the federal government (Article IV, Section 4). According to the Center for Immigration Studies, there are over 200 cities, counties and states that are sanctuaries based on their respective policies that forbid cooperation with ICE. None of them is being pursued by the DOJ.

President Obama's and Attorney General Holder's position on nullifying immigration law by opposing deportation, endorsing executive amnesty and encouraging invasion is unconstitutional and even treasonous in its scope. It is worse than an abdication of a constitutional duty; they are principals to crime by encouraging an invasion of illegal aliens including the 75,000 + reported "juveniles" from Central America sent through the Mexican border in June of 2014.

The Occupation Government (Administrative State) is at war with America. Immigration (legal and illegal) is one of its weapons. It is being used to introduce deadly and disabling diseases once eradicated here, terrorists, and violent criminals including sexual predators, economic sabotage and the dilution of the dominant culture. The lack of quality and quantity control on immigration is intentionally reckless, but sold to us as compassion.

We are not the virtuous, educated and informed people our founding fathers required us to be. If we were we would be outraged. We would have demanded impeachment proceedings in order to bring the abuse of power by the executive branch under Obama to light. Indeed, the abuse was so blatant and the damage so extreme that we would have invited a military coup (d'état) to restore the U.S. Constitution.

We would have then celebrated the successful use of the constitutional mechanisms at our disposal to have Obama peacefully and lawfully removed from office and even jailed along with former Attorney General Eric Holder. But, predictably there was no accountability. The federal government unconstitutionally nullified immigration law and ignored the U.S. Constitution whenever it suited their agenda. The invasion continued until Trump's election. The destructive executive orders continued until Trump. The people behaved as ignorant sheep, and the media gave the rogue Obama regime a pass.

An example of an area where states could and should properly nullify federal law is the Affordable Care Act. The Supreme Court held that it was constitutional under the power of the federal government to tax under Article I, Section 8. This presents a problem because Article I, Section 7, Clause 1 known as the Origination Clause says that all bills for raising money must originate in the House of Representatives, not the Senate.

The Senate is where Senator Harry Reid took House Resolution 3590, the Service Members Home Ownership Tax Act of 2009, and played a shell game. He removed the content under the "amendment" process replacing it with the Affordable Care Act. His confederates in the Senate knew that if they played by the rules the bill would never have come out of the

House where as a tax it was constitutionally required to begin.

The Democrat Party has moved far beyond the classic arguments of liberal versus conservative surrounding how generous government should be. This is no longer JFK's Democrat Party — radical Marxists run the party now.

The daily operation of the Administrative State and the way the Affordable Care Act was unconstitutionally passed illustrate that Marxists are changing the very structure of government behind the Democrat label. Before Obama's overt efforts to "fundamentally transform" America – in part by taking over 1/6 of the economy through Obamacare – came three equally zealous Democrat Marxists: Woodrow Wilson who inspired the League of Nations (later to become the UN), FDR who gave us the New Deal, and LBJ who introduced the Great Society. The Democrat Party has embraced Marxist ideology for a long time, incrementally transforming the USA into the USSA.

Obama saw his pen as a scepter. His executive orders are Marxist fatwas. James Madison's safeguards enumerated in the Constitutional separation of powers did not withstand the personal edicts of Dictator Obama. Unchallenged, he consolidated unconstitutional and autocratic power in the Oval Office.

Obama blatantly and shamelessly refused to enforce or obey a whole host of federal laws: illegal entry into the United States, illegal armed incursions into the U.S. by Mexican Army personnel and drug cartel members, illegal alien VISA violations, federal drug laws (marijuana), the Defense of Marriage Act, selective and arbitrary non-enforcement of the tax laws (dozens of IRS employees not prosecuted nor fined for failure to pay back taxes owed, including Al Sharpton, Bill and Hillary Clinton and former Treasury Secretary Timothy Geithner), Obamacare and the 24 unconstitutional and unilateral executive changes to it.

Just looking at the vulnerability along our borders one must objectively conclude that Obama willfully and knowingly exhibited a treasonous neglect and deliberate disregard to the national sovereignty and territorial integrity of the United States of America. Yet Obama was not impeached nor removed from office because the Republican Party is filled with co-conspirators and cowards.

Social Security, Medicare and Obamacare are all socialist programs. They are parts of an enormous Administrative State (occupation government) lurching and lording over us. If you agree we have been steadily moving toward socialism domestically why would you think our international policy would not be doing the same?

As many as 70 members of the U.S. Congress are affiliated with the treasonous Democratic Socialists of America (DSA), a sub-group of the Socialist International that actively and subversively works to destroy the independence and national sovereignty of the United States and ultimately submerge our country into an all-powerful, one-world totalitarian government (this is clearly on display with our unprotected open borders, the total lack of border enforcement, the stripping of Border Patrol agents' powers to apprehend and deport illegal aliens, and the various sovereignty-destroying international treaties, partnerships and "agreements" of the last 70 years).

Mikhail Gorbachev called the EU "the new European Soviet" and observed its rule by ex-communists. The U.S. is merging economies through Trans-Pacific partnerships in the same way. The Affordable Health Care Act is designed to offer rationed health care to the evolving North America Union (the merger of three populations and economies: Canada, the U.S., and Mexico). NAFTA/GATT/WTO/CAFTA came first. Then came Obamacare, and soon was to come amnesty for illegal aliens, and the Trans-Pacific Partnership (further integrating national economies to be co-dependent), and the Law of the Sea Treaty (LOST).

If Communism is our natural enemy why do China and Vietnam enjoy most-favored-trading status? Trump saved the day by turning the tables on all of this. Say what you will about his style, the man's policies put America first.

Trump challenges the status quo. His first order of business as president was to reject the Paris Accord. He knows we are living under an occupation government (The Administrative State) that is steered by an international communist agenda. President Trump speaking to the UN in October of 2018 rejected the Obama Administration's buy-in to placing us under the purview of international courts and tribunals with the Supreme Court of the United States no longer "supreme."

We were cautioned about government corruption and the consequences of societal devolution by our founders. We were told that our Republic depends on a virtuous, educated and informed people to survive.

We are rotting from within. We need a restoration. This cannot be done in the noxious cloud of moral relativism and ignorance promoted by the architects of the Diversity Movement. The founders gave us the means to fix our problems, but we lack the knowledge and will to do the hard things. President Trump cannot fix this alone.

It is for each of us to decide — today — if we take an active role in the short time we have left and restore our Constitutional Republic through interposition, nullification, recall elections and voting out of office the corrupt.

There is growing support for a Constitutional Convention ("Con-Con"), and this makes me nervous because it could open up the document to potentially dangerous changes that could deal a death blow to individual freedom and national sovereignty. We simply need to strip away the Administrative State and enforce the Constitution we have. We need to behave like citizens, not subjects! We must find and actively support bold candidates, who understand what is and is not Law; who know the purpose of government, its fixed standards, and will honor their oath.

Thomas Jefferson said, "When the government fears the people, there is liberty. When the people fear the government there is tyranny."

There is no doubt at this point in history that the (informed) American people fear their government. A police state was not the intention of the founders or the purpose of modern policing.

Sir Robert Peel is known as the "Father of Modern Policing." His Peelian Principles became the foundation of the Metropolitan Police Force of London.

Peelian # 7:

"Police, at all times, should maintain a relationship with the public that gives reality to the historic tradition that the police are the public and the public are the police; the police being only members of the public who are paid to give full-time attention to duties which are incumbent upon every citizen in the interests of community welfare and existence."

Police are not to replace the citizens' role in maintaining law and order, but to complement it. When London considered establishing a police force, the public's concern was that a police state would evolve that would be "...a curse and despotism..."

Sir Peel's nine principles were made to appease a worried public. Principle #7 acknowledged that the citizen was no less responsible for protecting the community than an officer. Furthermore, citizens are not below the police.

The 2005 Minutemen Project on the US/Mexico border; armed Korean store owners on the roofs of their businesses during the 1992 LA riots; militia in Ferguson (August 2015), following violence at the year anniversary of the justifiable police shooting death of violent Michael Brown; and armed members of Oath Keepers in front of National Guard recruiting offices (July 2015) to protect our unarmed guardsmen from terrorist attack – these are all lawful, and they are and consistent with Peelian principle # 7. Of course, the federal government views such an expression of grassroots freedom and responsibility as a threat to their evolving tyranny. That arrogant governing attitude is the antithesis of Peelian Principle # 7.

One only has to look at the ominous acquisition of military equipment and hardware by local police forces and federal law enforcement entities, as well as the prolific stockpiling of millions upon millions of rounds of ammunition by alphabet federal agencies to recognize that something sinister is afoot — and it does not bode well for you or what little freedoms you have left.

Edmund Burke warned, "There is no safety for honest men but by believing all possible evil of evil men."

It is appropriate to close this chapter with some words from two heroes of the War of Independence, George Washington and Thomas Jefferson:

"A free people ought not only be armed and disciplined, but they should have sufficient arms and ammunition to maintain a status of independence from any who might attempt to abuse them, which would include their own government." (George Washington)

In a speech before the 1st United States Congress, our Nation's first president and military leader of the War of Independence – George Washington – stated the following:

"Firearms stand next in importance to the Constitution itself. They are the American peoples' liberty teeth and keystone under independence...From the day the pilgrims landed to the present day events prove that in order to ensure peace, security and happiness, the rifle and the pistol are equally indispensable...they deserve a place of honor with all that is good. When firearms go, all goes. We need them every hour."

"The greatest reason for the people to retain the right to keep and bear arms is, as a last resort, to protect themselves against tyranny in government." (Jefferson)

Never! Never! Never relinquish your right to bear arms!

CHAPTER NINE

Domestic Assault and Battery

Mandatory and pro-arrest policies regarding domestic violence has nearly eliminated officer discretion on the matter throughout the country. Fear of consequences for using discretion has officers in a headlock. In the face of institutionalized social justice few officers have the moral courage to exercise discretion resulting in many unnecessary arrests that damage the American family.

Scenario:

A woman has been drinking adult beverages throughout the evening. Her husband and she argue over finances. She walks to the car. He grabs her by the wrist in order to prevent her from driving drunk. She screams, pulls away and falls; twisting her ankle in the driveway while the children look on.

The neighbor calls 911. Upon arrival, officers separate the couple, and interview them individually. The woman is crying. She has a red mark on her wrist and a swollen ankle consistent with her account of events and those of the neighbor, husband, and children. The injuries are minor. She refuses medical attention.

There is no history of domestic violence on file between the couple and the "victim" does not want her husband arrested. With no regard to the victim's protest he is arrested for domestic battery and the *enhancement section* — for committing the "offense" in the presence of children.

This scenario illustrates how unnecessary arrests set in motion a chain of events more damaging than anything that took place prior to law enforcement being called: The husband is unnecessarily arrested in front of his family and neighbors. A NCO (No Contact Order) is issued forbidding him from seeing his kids and wife or contacting them by phone, text, mail or through a third-party. He has to pay for bond or will miss work. He must spend more money living out of the home or risk arrest and even more money for an attorney unless he qualifies for the public defender. He cannot possess a firearm or ammunition while the NCO stands — even though they are not evidence of the alleged crime. Peace officers sometimes seize these items stripping the defendant of his Second Amendment right without Due Process; as if a man is less deadly without a gun. Shouldn't his chainsaw, shoelaces, kitchen knives, hammers, dumbbells, and baseball bats be seized too?

The humiliation, family separation and financial burden brought about from unnecessary, social-justice-inspired arrests are a strain on the family.

Pro-arrest policies are adopted by law enforcement administrators out of fear of expensive tort claims, fear of the Feds de-funding grants and fear of bad press. Fear is inculcated in officers through yearly in-service training. Arresting for the slightest, explainable injury is fail-safe. In cases of mutual battery police are expected to identify the "primary aggressor" and make an arrest. That is usually the male even if he was defending himself from his hysterical wife by overpowering her attack. The wife can corroborate his story, but still an arrest is made and often times the enhancement charge stacked on top if children were anywhere they could have conceivably heard the quarrel. Stacked charges make an unnecessary arrest more likely to result in a plea. That is easy money for the state. This is how the game is played. The man is neutered and fleeced. The policies surrounding how these laws are enforced are bias against men and profitable to the system in court costs and fines. Actual evidence matters less in domestic assault and battery than any other kind of crime.

Pro-arrest policies cause officers to not think. One size fits all. They pass the buck to prosecutors, placing them in an untenable position. Many of these cases are resolved by a plea to the lesser charge of disturbing the peace. The majority of defendants take a plea deal often times only to expedite the reunification of family, the restoration of rights, and stop the financial bleeding of separation and attorney fees. At $300.00 an hour for an attorney, how much "justice" can the average person afford?

In 2003, twenty-one-year-old Angie Leon of Nampa, Idaho, was murdered by her estranged husband,

Abel Leon — a known criminal alien. Over a five-year period, Abel Leon had fifty-nine contacts with law enforcement; almost all resulted in arrest. Thirty-five of the fifty-nine were for domestic violence.

Angie told authorities numerous times Abel would kill her. Angie's murder was as much the result of the failure of ICE as it was the prosecutor's office for not fighting to keep Abel in custody after a felony charge of eluding police — despite priors for three failure-to-appear warrants, twenty protection order violations and the state's knowledge he was a danger. ICRMP (Idaho's self-insured communities risk management plan) paid out $925,000 to Angie's mother, Sylvia Flores.

Cases like Leon are rightfully referenced in domestic violence training, but to such an extreme that the interests of city and county Risk Management offices have collided with justice, leaving a chalk line around discretion.

In 2011, there were seventeen deaths in Idaho related to domestic violence. Like Angie, those victims were not saved by domestic violence laws and pro-arrest policies. In fact, there is no way to know if domestic violence laws and the elimination of officer discretion reduce the number of injuries and murders or contribute to them — by holding victims hostage to their circumstances. Could a victim's past experiences with overzealous arrest policies and prosecution make her less likely to call 911 when all she wants is for officers to preserve the peace while she collects her toothbrush and leaves?

The argument in support of domestic violence laws is built on the premise that the pre-existing, non-tailored misdemeanor and felony assault and battery laws are insufficient given the unique psychological aspects of a (female) victim trapped in a cycle of domestic violence. The state argued it needed more power to intercede and prosecute on behalf of women paralyzed by fear, confusion and control.

Sometimes the state does know best. Nonetheless, **very few cases prosecuted as domestic assault or battery fit the kinds of controlling abuse that**

proponents of the law argued it was intended to address.

The pre-existing (and now co-existing) assault and battery laws are sufficient tools in the hands of competent peace officers empowered with discretion.

What makes matters worse is when the unwilling victim turns hostile to an overzealous arrest/prosecution and recants saying she lied to police. In an already weak case that should have been declined, this makes it difficult to prosecute a future (legitimate) case because the victim's credibility is damaged.

In addition, the underlying premise for the law may be flawed. The media ignore studies like, Domestic Violence: The Male Perspective, where research supports: "Domestic violence is often seen as a female victim/male perpetrator problem, but the evidence demonstrates that this is a false picture." This and other studies show men are nearly as often the victims of domestic violence (40%) as are women, but they under report.

I watched this area of law and police policy evolve from its inception in San Diego, California. It became the national model. Today, across the country domestic violence assault and battery laws are redundant and *gender biased* in their investigation and prosecution. In the absence of compelling physical evidence or an independent witness, "trained" police are left with one person's word against the other.

Police taught to value a woman's statement as having more veracity than a man's statement is no different than valuing the statement of a white over a black or the rich over the poor.

There is no doubt that good has come from some of these arrests, but that does not change my opinion that across the country (and in other Western countries) domestic violence laws are unnecessary and over zealously enforced. Too often these arrests damage the families they are purported to protect.

Compounding the damage to the family is the double standard found in the kinds of injuries that distinguish a misdemeanor domestic battery from a felony domestic battery; they are lower — and far more subjective — than the kinds of injuries that typically distinguish non-domestic misdemeanor batteries from non-domestic felony (male-on-male) batteries. The injury threshold for a man to be charged with felony domestic battery is far lower than the injury threshold for the same man being charged with felony battery from a common street fight.

The existing statutes for misdemeanor battery, misdemeanor assault, aggravated (felony) battery, aggravated (felony) assault, stalking, phone harassment and intimidating a witness are sufficient to address the very real issue of spouse-on-spouse, and other intimate partner assaults and batteries.

Repealing domestic violence law is unlikely. What is the alternative? Restore discretion.

The relative autonomy of the Office of Sheriff is pivotal in modeling this change. Yes, the feds could investigate and prosecute a select few cases under federal domestic violence law. Yes, the Department of Justice could de-fund grants to Sheriffs who honor their oath and row against the federally adopted, radical feminist narrative. Yes, the press will spin the move toward discretion casting the Sheriff a Neanderthal. So be it.

Sheriff, did you take the job to be popular or to honor your oath?

Most Sheriffs and Police Chiefs take the path of least resistance for fear of the potential negative consequences of being controversial. Going with the flow is damaging enough. Others take it a step beyond. In Canyon County, Idaho, Sheriff Kieran Donahue plays the domestic violence mantra to his political advantage by promoting his *Man Up Crusade Against Domestic Violence*. It sounds so unobjectionable. Domestic violence is as safe an issue to tie your reelection campaign to as anything that is for the children. There are purple ribbons, purple bandanas, purple stickers, purple t-shirts, rodeos and lots of positive free media coverage of the Sheriff who promotes a compassionate, zealous and *gender bias* message that in my view endorses the devastating absence of discretion by police in our homes.

Peace officers are the gatekeepers of who goes to jail. Decisions based on facts, reason and discretion must be restored. By department policy, a decision to not arrest for domestic battery could require a second opinion from a sergeant. Short of a crime report, an information report could be filed in-house describing what happened and why an arrest was not made. Such a report could be useful for call history in the event that some unforeseen tragedy does happen.

The existing pro-arrest practice aimed at eliminating all exposure to liability by making unnecessary arrests is fear driven; it advances a Marxist objective to damage the smallest form of government: the family.

The discretion I advocate is not license for peace officers to be lazy and leave a scene when they should make an arrest. Until crystal balls are issued to peace officers, *reason and facts*, not fear of special interest groups, tort claims and bad press — should steer their actions in our homes.

Quotes to ponder

"Democracy is the road to socialism."

– Karl Marx

"Politicians are the lowest form of life on earth. Liberal Democrats are the lowest form of politicians."

– General George S. Patton

"Democracies have ever been spectacles of turbulence and contention, have ever been found incompatible with personal security or the rights of property, and have in general been as short in their lives as they have been violent in their deaths."

– James Madison, "Father of the U.S. Constitution"

"Democracy never lasts long. It soon wastes, exhausts, and murders itself." – Samuel Adams

"There was never a democracy that did not commit suicide."

– John Adams

"Real liberty is never found in despotism or in the extremes of democracy." – Alexander Hamilton (Signer of the U.S. Constitution & co-author of the Federalist Papers)

"Democracy means simply the bludgeoning of the people by the people for the people." – Oscar Wilde

"Damn democracy. It is a fraudulent term used, often by ignorant persons but no less often by intellectual fakers, to describe an infamous mixture of socialism, graft, confiscation of property and denial of personal rights to individuals whose virtuous principles make them offensive."
– Westbrook Pegler

"A democracy is nothing more than mob rule, where fifty-one percent of the people may take away the rights of the other forty-nine."
– Thomas Jefferson

"If Congress can determine what constitutes the general welfare and can appropriate money for its advancement, where is the limitation to carrying into execution whatever can be effected by money?"

– South Carolina Senator William Draden, 1828

"The State is the great fiction by which everyone seeks to live at the expense of everyone else."

– Frederic Bastiat

"A democracy cannot exist as a permanent form of government. It can only exist until the voters discover that they can vote themselves largesse from the public treasury. From that moment on, the majority always votes for the candidates promising the most benefits from the public treasury, with the result that a democracy always collapses over loose fiscal policy, always followed by a dictatorship."

– Alexis de Tocqueville

"When men get in the habit of helping themselves to the property of others, they cannot easily be cured of it."
– The New York Times, in a 1909 editorial opposing the very first income tax.

"The average age of the world's greatest civilizations from the beginning of history has been about 200 years. During those 200 years, these nations always progressed through the following sequence: From bondage to spiritual faith; From spiritual faith to great courage; from courage to liberty; From liberty to abundance; From abundance to selfishness; From selfishness to complacency; From complacency to apathy; From apathy to dependence; From dependence back into bondage."

    – Alexander Fraser Tytler, The Fatal Sequence

"No society that has been reorganized and restructured to provide such a perverse system of incentives deserves to survive, indeed, no such civilized society ever has survived. The collapse of American empire is precisely what will bring about the end of the current system in which the unproductive prosper on the efforts of the productive, and it is certain because it is mathematically unsustainable."

– Vox Day

"Pure democracy is a chimera – all government is essentially of the nature of a monarchy. The people flatter themselves that they have the sovereign power. These are, in fact, words without meaning. It is true they elected governors – but how are these elections brought about? In every instance of election by the mass of a people – through the influence of those governors themselves, and by means the most opposite to a free and disinterested choice, by the basest corruption and bribery. But those governors once selected, where is the boasted freedom of the people?

They must submit to their rule and control, with the same abandonment of their natural liberty, the freedom of their will, and the command of their actions, as if they were under the rule of a monarch."

– Alexander Fraser Tytler

"If the Tenth Amendment were still taken seriously most of the federal government's present activities would not exist. That's why no one in Washington ever mentions it."

– Thomas Woods

"No modern president has picked and chosen which laws to enforce and which to ignore and which to rewrite to the extremes of President Obama. His radical rejection of the 'Rule of Law'...presents a clear and present danger to the freedom of us all."

– Judge Andrew Napolitano

"It does not take a majority to prevail...but rather an irate, tireless minority, keen on setting brushfires of freedom in the minds of men."   Samuel Adams (Signer of the Declaration of Independence)

"Timid men prefer the calm of despotism to the tempestuous sea of liberty."

– Thomas Jefferson

"If you will not fight for right when you can easily win without bloodshed; if you will not fight when your victory will be sure and not too costly; you may come to the moment when you will have to fight with all the odds against you and only a precarious chance of survival. There may even be a worse case. You may have to fight when there is no hope of victory, because it is better to perish than live as slaves."

– Winston Churchill

"The hour is fast approaching, on which the Honor and Success of this army and the safety of our bleeding Country depend. Remember, officers and soldiers, that you are Free Men, fighting for the blessings of Liberty – that slavery will be your portion, and that of your posterity, if you do not acquit yourselves like Men."

– George Washington, General Orders, August 23, 1776

"The time is now near at hand which must probably determine whether Americans are to be Freemen or Slaves; whether they are to have any property they can call their own; whether their houses and farms are to be pillaged and destroyed, and they consigned to a state of wretchedness from which no human efforts will probably deliver them. The fate of unborn millions will now depend, under God, on the courage and conduct of this army. Our cruel and unrelenting enemy leaves us only the choice of brave resistance, or the most abject submission. We have, therefore, to resolve to conquer or die."

– General George Washington, Speaking to his troops before the Battle of Long Island, New York, August 27, 1776

"The strongest reason for the people to retain their right to keep and bear arms is, as a last resort, to protect themselves against tyranny in government."

– Thomas Jefferson

"A free people ought not only be armed and disciplined, but they should have sufficient arms and ammunition to maintain a status of independence from any who might attempt to abuse them, which would include their own government."

"Firearms stand next in importance to the Constitution itself. They are the American peoples' liberty teeth and keystone under independence...When firearms go, all goes. We need them every hour."

– George Washington

"To preserve liberty, it is essential that the whole body of the people always possess arms and be taught alike, especially when young, how to use them."

– Colonel Richard Henry Lee, militia commander during the War of Independence

"To disarm the people is the best and most effectual way to enslave them."

– George Mason, author of the Second Amendment

"When government takes away citizens' right to bear arms it becomes citizens' duty to take away government's right to govern."

– George Washington

"Today, we need a nation of Minutemen, citizens who are not only prepared to take arms, but citizens who regard the preservation of freedom as the basic purpose of their daily life and who are willing to consciously work and sacrifice for that freedom."

– John F. Kennedy (over 50 years ago)

"The duty of a true Patriot is to protect his country from its government."

– Thomas Paine

"In the long history of the world, very few generations have been granted the role of defending freedom in its maximum hour of danger. This is that moment and you are that generation! Now is the time to defend our freedoms."

– Judge Andrew Napolitano

"Nothing can now be believed which is seen in a newspaper. Truth itself becomes suspicious by being put into that polluted vehicle. The real extent of this state of misinformation is known only to those who are in situations to confront facts within their knowledge with the lies of the day."

– Thomas Jefferson, 1807

"If voting made any difference they wouldn't let us do it."

– Mark Twain

"It is no measure of health to be well-adjusted to a profoundly sick society."   – Jiddu Krishnamurti

INDEX

Abandoned Property _____ 48
Apparent Authority _____ 36
Arizona v. Gant _____ 35
Arrests _____ 22, 25, 29
Arrest Warrants _____ 27, 42
Automobile Exception to search warrant _____ 29
Citizen's Arrest _____ 24, 33
Community Caretaking Exception _____ 39
Consensual Contacts _____ 10
Consent Searches _____ 35
Detentions _____ 11
Distinguishing Chimel from Terry _____ 18
Exigent Circumstances Exceptions _____ 37
Flight _____ 6, 11
Fresh Pursuit _____ 40
Knock and Announce _____ 47
Misdemeanors Officers can arrest for when not committed in their presence _____ 24
Open View Doctrine _____ 28
Plain Feel _____ 5
Plain View Doctrine _____ 28, 48
Pretext Stops _____ 17
Probable Cause _____ 1, 3, 4, 45
Protective Frisk on Warrant Service _____ 22
Protective Searches of Vehicles _____ 18
Protective Sweeps _____ 20
Reasonable Suspicion _____ 3
School Searches _____ 40
Search Incident to Arrest _____ 32, 35
Search Warrants _____ 45
Temporal Issue _____ 33
Terry v. Ohio _____ 4
Tracking Devices _____ 48
Traffic Stops _____ 15
Trunks _____ 32, 39
Vehicle Inventory Exception _____ 39
Warrantless Entry _____ 7, 26, 27, 38
Warrantless Search _____ 23, 28, 29, 40, 42

www.ingramcontent.com/pod-product-compliance
Lightning Source LLC
Chambersburg PA
CBHW030648220526
45463CB00005B/1683